Upon Silver Wings II

World-Record Adventure

CAROLANN GARRATT

INCLUDING SOME EMAILS AND JOURNAL ENTRIES BY CAROL M. FOY

Barbara —
It was a pleasure
to meet you at KTTA.
Blue skies,
[signature] 6/17/09

Gainesville, Florida

UPON SILVER WINGS II
World-Record Adventure
by CarolAnn Garratt

First Edition
Editor: Rick "Gilligan" Uschold, Liza Weaver, Arthur Miller, Carol M. Foy
Book Design: Janice Phelps Williams (www.janicephelps.com)

ISBN-13: 978-0-9753457-6-4
ISBN-10: 0-9753457-6-1

Website: www.alsworldflight.com
To order additional copies of *Upon Silver Wings II*,
please see the order form at the back of the book.

Cover photograph by Joe Burbank, reproduced with
approval from the *Orlando Sentinel* and our thanks.
Other photographs by Dave and Lyn Berelsman, Tony Martin, Robin
Caple, Katherine Scheer-Perry and Louis Smyth from Universal Weather,
Chris Cooper, Tadthai 'Bo' Praichan, Jim Buchan, Debey Von,
Kerry Rhodes, Charles Cooper, Norm Livingstone, Dennis Fujimoto,
Nancy Warren, and Carol Foy.

Disclaimer
Statements contained herein are the opinions of CarolAnn Garratt and
may contain inadvertent errors. No warranty of accuracy or factual
completeness is either expressed or implied. Discussions of flight procedures are meant to be of an informal and conversational nature only and
do not necessarily represent the views of the aviation authorities of any
government. Furthermore, nothing herein should be construed as ground
or flight instruction. Also note that long, transoceanic flying carries with it
significant risks necessitating special training and the carriage of sophisti-
cated navigation and survival equipment. Such flights should never be
attempted without proper preparation.

This flight is dedicated to our co-pilots in spirit:
Andy Garratt, brother of CarolAnn, died in a plane accident
in January 2006. Bob Foy, husband of Carol, died of cancer in
April 2004. Each would have been our chosen co-pilot
had they still been with us.

Andy Garratt

Bob Foy

This book is dedicated to our family members afflicted with ALS.
CarolAnn's mother died of ALS in April 2002. Carol's cousin,
Hal has had ALS for 5 years and is doing the best he can.

Marie Garratt

Hal Stoltz

All donations for books go directly to ALS Therapy Development
Institute, the world's leading scientific lab working only on
finding the cause and cure to ALS.

The Dash —

I read of a man who stood to speak
at the funeral of a friend.
He referred to the dates on her tombstone
from the beginning...to the end.

He noted that first came the date of her birth
and spoke of the following date with tears,
but he said what mattered most of all
was the dash between those years.

For that dash represents all the time
that she spent alive on earth...
and now only those who loved her
know what that little line is worth.

For it matters not, how much we own;
the cars....the house...the cash.
What matters is how we live and love
and how we spend our dash.

So think about this long and hard...
are there things you'd like to change?
For you never know how much time is left
that can still be rearranged.

If we could just slow down enough
to consider what's true and real,
and always try to understand
the way other people feel.

And be less quick to anger,
and show appreciation more
and love the people in our lives
like we've never loved before.

If we treat each other with respect,
and more often wear a smile...
remembering that this special dash
might only last a little while.

So, when your eulogy is being read
with your life's actions to rehash...
would you be proud of the things they say
about how you spend your dash?

Please see a wonderful rendition of
The Dash at: www.thedashmovie.com/linda

TABLE OF CONTENTS

Carol Foy and CarolAnn Garratt
The start.

Completion of the 8-day
around-the-world Dash
for a Cure

Photo by Joe Burbank,
reprinted with approval
from the Orlando Sentinel

ACKNOWLEDGMENTS

This flight and world record would not have been possible without the support and help of hundreds of people worldwide.

Friends of friends of friends along with corporate colleagues I hadn't spoken with in several years offered help and support with many different aspects of the preparation and flight. Carol had excellent contacts at Mooney and elsewhere who also helped enormously.

We would like to thank everyone who supported us to make this flight a success.

Engine: Arthur Miller did the annual inspection and replaced all the accessories in June 2008, 100 hours prior to the flight. In addition, he did some major "what if analysis" during the inspection of the aircraft to make sure all bases had been covered. He did the final 100-hour inspection just prior to the December departure. Gene Svoboda did the engine overhaul in 2005, with full knowledge that it would be doing another around-the-world flight. He gave the engine a "once over" in July 2008.

Communication: Wes and Sandy Whitley installed the High Frequency radio gear and trailing antenna as well as lending their radio and data unit for the trip. This is an extremely important part of oceanic flight. Wes also designed a cockpit voice recorder so that we could capture all the intercom and ATC communications around the world. Sandy designed and made a custom pillow to improve rest during the flight. Wes also handled the web site updating to keep everyone informed during the flight.

Flight planning assistance: Putting the route together would not have been possible without people in many countries with ATC contacts and experience: Norman Livingstone, Saudamini Deshmukh, Flemming and Angela Pedersen, Bill and Sue Harrelson, Jim Nisbet, Lauren Stroschin, Tony Smith, Gerald Cooper, John Foster, Tom Benson, Tim Cornelison, Charles Cooper, Elsie Quenga, Theresa White, and Paul Arrambide. Bo Therkildsen in Denmark spent months getting the over-flight and landing permits. In addition he worked tirelessly the week prior to and during the flight to insure all permits and deviations went smoothly.

Fuel system: Mark Vanbenschoten, Arthur Miller, and Al Kimball.

Weather forecasting and ground handling: Universal Weather offered their support very early in the planning. We appreciate the 24-hour support of Foxtrot Team including Judd Karnilow, Jerri Banks, Paula Acosta, Suzanne Goldman, and Tami Kepner with weather expertise from Dave, Mike, and Randall.

Regional Ground crews: Bill Harrelson in the US, Norman Livingstone in Thailand, and Flemming Pedersen in Switzerland were our regional ground crews handling receipt and analysis of weather, confirmation of flight plans and timing, and communication with us while flying. They allowed us to minimize our ground time by having all decisions made ahead of time while we were flying.

Local ground crews: Most stops had a local ground crew that we'd contacted ahead of time to facilitate our turnaround time. In San Diego, brother, Richard Garratt, and earthrounder, Jay Showers, along with Ann Pooch and airport operations Chris Cooper kept us going. In Hawaii, Scott Allen contacted Roger Caple, who replenished us, and airport manager, George Crabbe. In Guam, Charles Cooper of Care Jet looked after us with ATC coordination by Tim Cornelison. At our major maintenance stop in Chiang Mai, Thailand, Norm Livingstone coordinated with the agents at Nok and SGA (Siam General Aviation) and we were taken under the wing of Tadthai 'Bo' Praichan. In Cape Verde the SafePort crew were excellent. In Orlando, Florida, for our departure and arrival at Galaxy Aviation, Michelle and team were very helpful.

Video: Kabir Chuttani, doctor/pilot/photographer joined the support of ALS and the flight by recommending video taping during the flight and providing his camera. He made a special trip to Florida for the first installation and test in October then a second trip in November to finalize details for the camera and flight.

Fundraising: It was a terrific event and a good idea, but the timing of the economy was the worst possible for philanthropy. In addition to the ALS personnel, Dave McKanna and Alicia Favicchio our volunteer fundraisers included Ronnie Weston, Kabir Chuttani, and many employees from Fusion PR in New York City, Stephen Andrews, Suzanne McGee, and Meghan O'Hara. MAPA, Mooney Aircraft Pilots Association gave us tremendous support during EAA AirVenture in Oshkosh, WI. Our local Orlando marketing team and fundraisers include Dave and Lyn Berelsman and Chris Fenger.

Borrowed items:
We couldn't have done this without many items which were lent or donated including: a pulse oximeter from Marcia Gitelman, charts from Saudamini and Peter, a transponder initially from Fred Weaver and ultimately from Art Hanold, HF equipment from Wes and Sandy Whitley, Panasonic video camcorder from Kabir Chuttani, a flight timer from Tony Yacono, a drum opening wrench from Stone Petroleum, tools from Art Miller, head rests from Blaine Hoffman, oxygen dosimeter from Joe Colonna, a flight tracker from TracPlus, a life jacket from Tom Seng, and the tanks from Mark Vanbenschoten.

Although two women sat in the plane for 204 hours to set a new world record, we couldn't have done it without you all.

We sincerely appreciate all your help and support. Thank you. We hope through this flight and book we can encourage and inspire others to live life, learn and share.

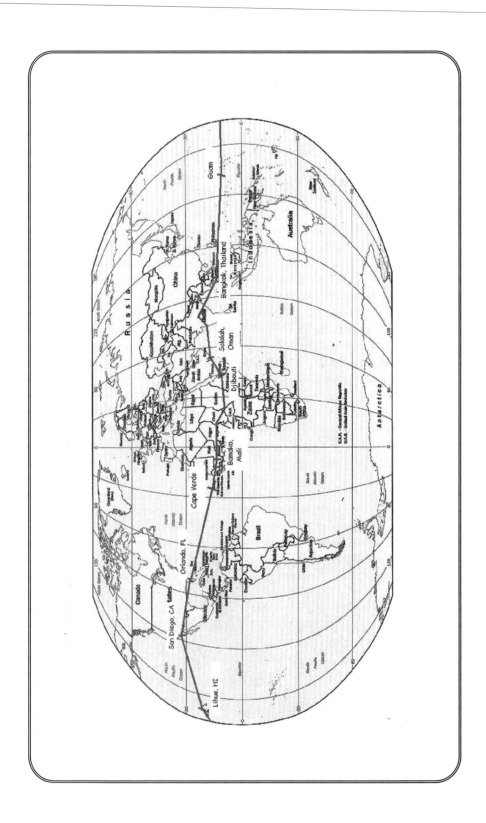

Departure, KMCO,[*] Orlando International Airport

KSDM, San Diego Brown Municipal Airport

PHLI, Lihue Airport

PGUM, Guam International

VTCC, Chiang Mai, Thailand

OOSA, Salalah, Oman

HDAM, Djibouti

GABS, Bamako, Mali

GVAC, Sal, Cape Verde Islands

Return, KMCO, Orlando International Airport

---

[*] KMCO. All airports, worldwide, have four-letter identifiers. KMCO is the identifier for the Orlando International Airport in Orlando, FL.

In 2003 Carolann took her Mooney on a 7-month journey around the world and wrote her first book to

raise donations for ALS research.
Cover and map from
Upon Silver Wings: Global Adventure in a Small Plane

"A daughter's tribute to her mother takes her to the skies.
It's an around-the-world journey of love and purpose —
to raise awareness of the disease that claimed her mom's life."
–Orlando Sentinel, 2003

INTRODUCTION

Following my 2003 world flight, I started making presentations to flying clubs and EAA chapters and telling them about my flight and ALS. During this time, I took the website and turned it into a book, *Upon Silver Wings*. It's hard to believe that five years have passed since that flight. Much of the time, I took care of my 80+-year-old father, who came to live with me in 2005. But, in the spring of 2007, I started planning this adventure.

I was actually planning a three-year around-the-world, slow flight to visit countries and meet people. However, my dad was still with me at the time and I couldn't see how it would be possible. But, the idea of a "quick" flight came to my mind. Actually, the idea may have been in my mind for a long time. Re-reading the last sentences of the Epilogue of *Upon Silver Wings,* I wrote, "Then, after running the new engine for a year, we'll be ready to go again! With a new prop, good weather, and a little luck, maybe we could even try for a speed record... me and my Mooney."

Also, I have a picture in my mind of me pouring over an atlas at my dad's home in Virginia. I was trying to figure out the minimum number of stops to make it around the world. This must have been back in 2004. So, this idea has been simmering beneath my conscious memory for a while.

Since May 2007 I've been working towards the goal of flying around the world in seven days and raising one million dollars for ALS research.

Photo crew with Carol and CarolAnn at Orlando International Airport

CHAPTER 1
FINDING A CO-PILOT

 July/August 2007 — Choosing a Co-pilot

As I worked on the planning, I had a piece of paper on the side of my desk with the heading: Co-pilot. As I thought of a potential copilot, I'd put his/her name on the list. My brother, Richard, was on the list, but scratched through as I didn't think it appropriate for him to do this with a six-year-old daughter at home. Several other women pilots' names were on the list. They had different experiences from being airline pilots to relatively new pilots with different overseas experience. Over time the list grew. Then one day I thought about Carol Foy. I knew immediately that she would be the best choice. Carol was a Mooney pilot, delivered and ferried Mooneys, raced in the Women's Air Race Classic, a good complement to my economy minded cruising, and lived on an air park with her Mooney. Everything she did was in the aviation vein; same as me.

Although I felt she was the right person, it took a while, with the list sitting on my desk, before I contacted her. I finally sent an email and held my breath.... Within two days, I received a reply: Subject to talking with her immediate family, she was up for the challenge; could we talk by phone over the next week to get a better understanding of the task? I was ecstatic. Now the detailed planning could really get underway and two heads would be better than one. I didn't want to get everything finalized before including the second pilot.

Email from Carol, 8/10/07
Well, I've have talked to my family and they haven't told

me no or that I'm crazy. Their main concern is who will take care of the dog if I don't come back.

Hmmmmm.....

Anyway, I have also talked to my friend Paul who has extensive international experience with Atlas and he helped me generate some of the questions. In thinking about this flight and route, my initial greatest fears are politics and fatigue, in that order. I will also be doing the flight to London with him next week – 12 hours en route – so I'll have a good bit more information as to my own tolerance/adaptation to fatigue and performance. Most of the other questions are logistics, and you may have a sense of the answers, but understandably perhaps not the answers yet.

So, I am interested, and talk to you in the am!

CF

We spoke at 11am EDT on August 11, 2007.

▸ Carol weighs 125 lbs, same as me, great start.

▸ As she mentioned in the email, fatigue was a prime worry, but she'd be doing the flight to London the following week and would have more information on her reactions.

▸ Sudan worried her; me too. I explained that we often only get the negative news and countries aren't always as bad as the news we receive. I was going to try to get more information about flying in Africa and find people to meet us at each stop.

▸ Ditching and ditching at night are a major consideration. We decided to try to find and take a ditching course.

▸ Sleep in the plane. As we each had a Mooney we decided that we could each practice in our own hangar.

▸ Video uplink; was that something we could envisage. I hadn't thought about it, but we'd look into it.

▸ Would we have all the charts with us or pick them up at each stop? Again, to be put on the list and be evaluated.

The following weekend, of August 18th, a call from out of the blue; I was ecstatic by the end of the conversation.

"Oh, yes, I remember you, Mark." I'd mailed a letter to him several weeks previously asking about tanking his Mooney. He said he had a 120-gallon tank that fit in place of the rear seats, and that he'd be happy to lend it to me, and he'd always received a 20% over gross signoff by the FAA. Wow, we hit the jackpot today. This was the news I needed to do the long legs over the Pacific Ocean and to go non-stop across the Atlantic.

> 8/19/07
> It was great to talk with you again. As I mentioned on the phone, Rick and I are planning to try and visit Santa [North Pole] in mid-April of 2008. If we don't manage to lose the Mooney somehow along the way, you're welcome to use the tanks for your next flight.
> Mark

Mark had already flown around the world and made one attempt to fly his Mooney to the North Pole. This spring he is going to try again.

> 8/21/07
> Concerning the tanks, you may want to consider using mine for the "dash" (assuming 120 gallons is a good number for what you have in mind) and then decide if you want to fabricate your own set for the longer flight with less/more capacity.
> Mark

That's when "the dash" came into being. From then on Carol and I referred to our flight as The Dash. Thanks Mark!

Meeting September 10-12th at Carol Foy's hangar-home in Spicewood, TX

The annual meeting of the 99s[*] (International Organization of Women Pilots) had been on my schedule for a year. It was to be in Denver in mid-September 2007 and I was to speak. I had it on my calendar to visit my friend, Cathy, in Ft. Collins, go to the presentation, and then return to Ft. Collins to fly Young Eagles.

Since Texas is on the way to Colorado (well, sort of), Carol and

---

[*] The Ninety-nines is the International Organization of Women Pilots started by 99 female pilots, including Amelia Earhart.

Carol M. Foy and her Mooney

I had planned to meet for a few days, discuss the trip, and see how we got along. I picked up an Angel Flight from Florida to Houston, dropped off the very thankful patient at the FBO and continued on to Spicewood Airport.

After the tour of Carol's small home in the corner of her hangar, we were both ready to get into details. The major change since our last discussion was that I'd obtained a 120-gallon tank for the rear seats which increased our endurance. I hadn't recalculated stops as I wanted us to do it together, reviewing distances, times, winds, and lengths of each leg. We spent a morning preparing an optimum track with an alternate route in case of weather, headwinds, or anything else. We'd cut out three stops or six hours as we were calculating an optimum turnaround time at two hours per stop. I'd wanted to stop in Thailand as I have friends there and wanted locals and people I could count on to meet us in each country. The optimum route has us stopping in Myanmar (formerly Burma), just next door to Thailand. And, that stop doesn't have avgas. So, I'll be contacting my friends to see what they think of using Rangoon and if it'll be possible to ship 200 gallons of avgas into the country. We also had issues with using Guam. Carol took that challenge. I'd look into using Midway, but our fallback position was Hawaii to Guam.

By stretching our legs over the Pacific and making a stop further west of Thailand, we'd be able to fly straight to Djibouti and skip the gas stop in India. Although I was hoping, with help from local pilots and 99s, the stop in India wouldn't be too difficult or bureaucratic. By skipping India, we would no longer have the concern of an excessively time-consuming gas stop. However, we'd still get visas and have the contingency in place in the event it became necessary.

I showed Carol the weather sites I was using, especially for forecast winds. We agreed that reviewing weather and winds on a daily basis during November and December, and keeping a log of the actual weather this year, as well as comparing it with historical data would be necessary to pick a final time frame for our trip.

Cockpit or crew resource management (CRM) was on my list for discussion. Carol was used to flying with two pilots in the cockpit. During the Air Races they always flew with two pilots and sometimes changed Pilot In Command (PIC) and flying/non-flying duties and sometimes retained the same duties throughout the race. She was also flying Second In Command (SIC) on a King Air and on a Swearingen jet. On the other hand, I just about always flew solo and was interested in CRM from her perspective. Carol explained how tasks were shared in various flights, what happened during emergencies, and where responsibilities lay. I had read an article by Martha King and was most interested in how the copilot told the flying pilot that he/she was uncomfortable about a situation and felt that something different needed to be done. Carol said that in Air Races, both pilots discussed such issues and reached an agreement. She hadn't had a major situation like that occur. I suggested that we find the article and hopefully a CRM course that we could both take.

On funding the flight, I explained that I was willing to pay all expenses; mainly avgas and any necessary capital expenses to get the plane ready for such a trip. But, that I wanted many of the aviation companies to make donations to ALS research. I thought that when buying new equipment, I could explain the world-record attempt to the company and suggest that my purchase price become a donation to ALS with another matching contribution by the company. In exchange they would be listed as a donor on the webpage covering the flight. We'd need a package explaining the world-record flight, cause, pilots, and credentials. We put that on our growing list of things to do.

It was a long day and we went out to dinner overlooking the river in Marble Falls, Texas. At one point, I asked Carol how she felt about life since the death of her husband, Bob.

I was moved by her openness, feelings, and beliefs. They were very similar to those of my sister-in-law who had lost her husband, my brother, 18 months previously. I had not yet told Carol about Andy's death and I couldn't bring myself to do it that evening. However, I had been fatalistic about my first world trip (believing that if anything happened and I was killed, the same thing would have happened if I'd been staying in Orlando, maybe a car accident or something) and now felt the same way about this trip. But, at the same time, it was beginning to feel right. The last trip had felt right all the time; it never felt risky or dangerous and the weather cooperated practically the whole way. Now, this trip was coming together and I had the feeling that it was meant to be and that it was going to be successful. We still had a long way to go.

The next morning we went flying. Believe it or not, I was nervous. This was a test to see if I was acceptable to Carol as a pilot on this trip. Even though I had over 1500 hours in my Mooney, I was apprehensive. We did challenge/response check lists and decided that should continue on future flights and on our trip. I did the flying and Carol did the radio and navigation to BAZ, New Braunfels, Texas. I usually use autopilot, but didn't on this trip and my heading drifted a little, but I stayed on altitude. My pattern started a little high, but I slowed down in time and did a reasonable landing. Not my best, but very acceptable.

During breakfast we continued our discussions and I got back to CRM and changing seats. I wasn't sure if I wanted to do this or not. Many pilots with equal qualifications alternate PIC and SIC duties and sitting in the left and right seats. Carol said that, yes, she felt we should do this. I was uncertain whether we could sleep in different seats or if we'd prefer one side (as I do on airline flights).

We also discussed airspeeds. Carol flies fast everywhere, as do most Mooney pilots. I have a more economical style of flying, set out early, arrive early, but use lower power settings and less fuel. I've done this for seven years and know my Mooney's performance.

Carol recommended that I start flying at higher power settings and start logging and calculating fuel consumption and true air speeds at different altitudes with these higher power settings. That made sense to me. I'd start on the next leg to Colorado.

Carol flew left seat on our return to Spicewood. I handled the radio and navigation. I found it difficult to just do "half the job" so to speak. But, with needing two pilots and needing rest, we'd both have to practice, talk through difficulties, and figure out how to make it work.

Carol did a superb landing back at her home airport. Yep, she was the right person to have on board for this trip. We each had our list from our two days of discussions. I gassed up and took off for Colorado.

October 4, 2007

Wow, this week a lot of things came together, making me feel good about the trip and planning. I emailed Carol with an update, but no response yet, she must be busy flying.

> 10/1/2007
>
> Hello Carol –
>
> I hope your trips are going well. After returning from CO, I went to VA to pick up my dad. He's back with me now, so no long trips until next year. Garmin is in for WAAS upgrade, so I'll start flying with that in a few weeks.
>
> I've been working mainly on my biplane, but since I'm waiting for dope to dry, I've done some more planning. Here's what I've done so far.
>
> Bad news from Midway, no go on avgas or storing it for us. The manager is going to ask the Fish and Wildlife Service, but it doesn't look good. Good news, Lihue, Hawaii, does have avgas!! There to Guam (3202 nm) is 22:31 hours, at 142 k, conservative, not counting tailwinds. At 156 knots with 15 knot tailwinds, almost 19 hours. We could have a decision point to make the

Marshall Islands if winds and TAS don't give us enough comfort.

I have friends stopping in two of our destinations in the next few months. I've asked for contacts, phone numbers, email, etc. One is in Mali. It looks much better than Niger; a good tourist country with avgas only 200 nautical miles further west.

Attached is a very rough cut at the info sheet to go to potential donors. When you have time, please edit critically and add your info. No rush, I wouldn't expect to go out until early next year. Hopefully I can see a lot of vendors at Sun 'N Fun and Oshkosh.

Other thoughts: fly over US at night... lighter winds but nothing to see... quieter for ATC also. Burma/Myanmar isn't looking good, so I'm back to Thailand with a stop in India.

I'll send Mark's email with description of space around tank. Sounds pretty tight. I'll try to get pics.

That's all so far. Take care,

CA

In addition to all that, I emailed Wes, HF guru and pilot/friend, with my plans; he was only the fifth person I'd told about the flight. He was excited and willing to help. He contracts for NASA and I asked if he had any contacts to advise us about exercises during the long flights, any issues with sitting for seven days, and about food recommendations for the trip.

I found some new weather sites showing weather patterns around the world, how they were moving, and five-day forecasts. This should help for picking a starting date and knowing most of the weather for two-thirds of the way around. The only unknowns would be across Africa and the Atlantic Ocean which are pretty consistent and predictable at that time of year.

I also heard from another contact who had flown around the world in a C-182 in 2003, Dean Stahr. He gave me the information on the company that got his clearances as he traveled. Wanting to keep an open start date, based on a five-day weather picture, it was a priority to use a company with good global contacts who could handle this type of trip and last-minute country permits.

Things are progressing well and we're still 14 months from takeoff!!

Over the years, I've spoken with other Earthrounders and they agree, half the fun is the planning. I really enjoy those moments when everything else around the house is done and I can pull out my maps and computer and get to work on the trip. This week was like that. Every day I was able to immerse myself in the planning: look at the countries' typical weather patterns, watch the winds across the oceans at 5000 and 10,000 feet, look up the planned airports' facilities and other information on various websites to cross check their avgas availability, fees, and customs availability. Sometimes I do the planning to the detriment of eating, cleaning the house, and doing the dishes.... But eventually they get done.

November 7, 2007

David Berelsman had flown and traveled with me for six weeks on my trip in 2003. We'd stayed in touch even after I left Orlando in 2004 to live in Ocala. I told him about the plans and asked him to keep it quiet. He code named the project "Capricorn." We met at Tailwinds Café at Ocala Airport and talked about Capricorn. He always has lots of ideas and is more of a marketing person than I. He loaned me Steve Fossett's autobiography, *Chasing the Wind,* to read and get more ideas. I left with a long list of ideas and an agreement to meet in Orlando with others for further development of the marketing and strategy.

November 23, 2007 — Difficult Days; things to think about

Dad died two days ago.... Not getting much done. Lying on the couch reading, working in the hangar a little, back to the couch. Printing out his obituary and writing letters to the people in his address book. Many old friends and family live in England and they exchange Christmas cards, so I don't have email addresses. I've already sent out emails to all the cousins in England and his sister and my cousins in New Zealand.... It's difficult.

I hadn't told him about this trip. I wasn't sure how he'd take the news. Now I can't tell him. I feel sad; I should have told him.... How he would have reacted is up to him, not me. I've heard people say they wish they'd told someone something, now they can't .... Now it's my turn.

Lots to do and not in the mood to get anything done. I know I'll get over this feeling in a few weeks, but right now I don't feel like doing anything.

A few days ago I checked and saved the winds and weather around the world. I need to do that again. As we plan to go next November/December, I want to start gathering that data to see what it will look like at this time of year. Last week there was a low going across the North Atlantic, making headwinds for our crossing! That's unusual, we'll have to avoid that next year. There was also a favorable front west of Asia giving nice easterly winds with no rain in the southern Asian region. Let's hope that continues. I'll check again.

Just thinking about it and writing helps me to feel better. It's an empty feeling, a loss — it happens to everyone, but it hurts when it happens. I'd been taking care of Dad for three years, so he was part of the household. I was mad at times as he'd taken my freedom away from me. I couldn't go on trips, I couldn't get away. But now I miss him. He's actually the cause of this trip!! Well, indirectly. I was planning my next long trip, but with taking care of Dad it was going to be a while before I could execute my planning, so I thought about a QUICK trip.... That's how this idea, to do a world-record flight, emerged. I really wish I'd told him.

He knows now... He's up there, along with Mum and Andy, my brother, and Carol's husband, Bob, and they'll all watch over us during the planning and the flight. Now, back to work....

December 15, 2007

I've been watching the winds around the world along our route on most days, watching the forecasts and the pressure movements. It's looking pretty consistent. Early in the month there was a late low pressure moving across the Atlantic giving headwinds where we would expect tailwinds; that was unusual. Across the Pacific there have been consistent tailwinds but sometimes further south of our anticipated track. Both of these legs will have alternates just in case the winds aren't in our favor the day we are traveling. One of the weather sites gives a five-day forecast. If we can watch that and get all our permits at the last minute, we'll be pretty sure of our weather for two-thirds of the trip, leaving only Africa and the Atlantic to chance.

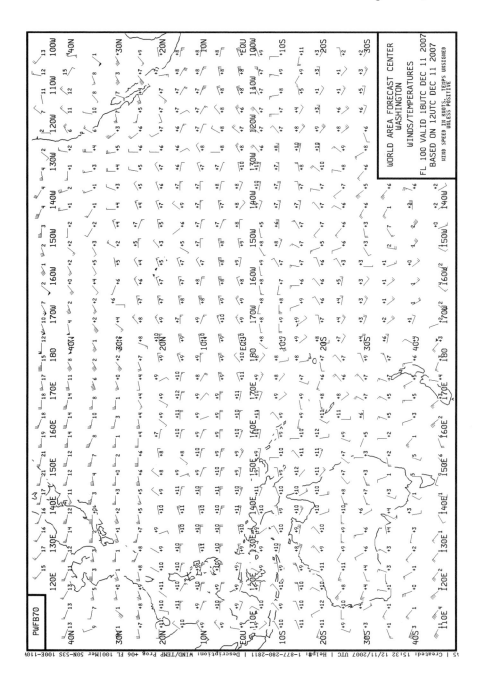

Pacific Winds: very consistent from ENE from 10 to 20 knots

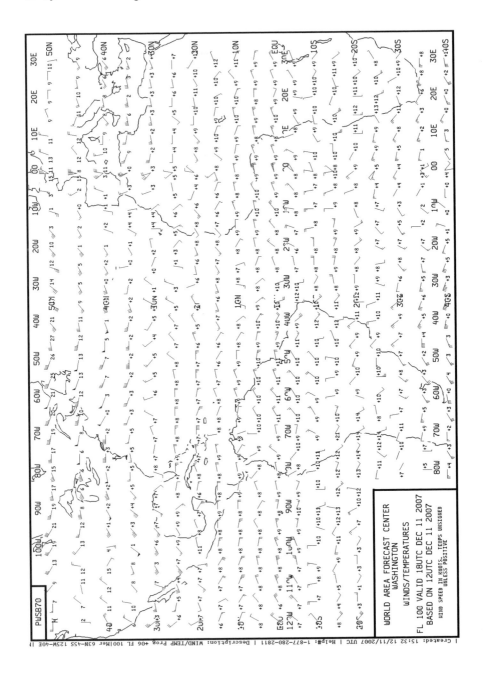

Atlantic Winds: fairly consistent from E for most of the crossing.
Expecting some headwinds for the final few hundred miles

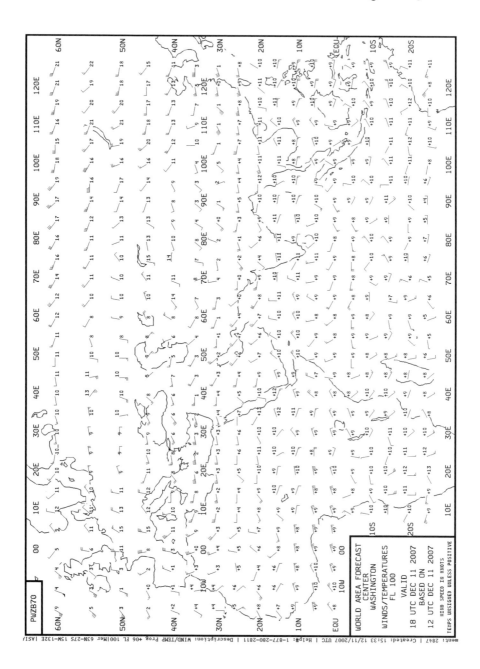

India/Africa Winds: Winds consistently easterly at 10N latitude and 15N latitude; changeable further to the north.

December 27, 2007 — Live Oak, FL

Sue and Bill are early-retired airline pilots, homebuilders, and plane/flying crazy. We struck up a friendship from our first meeting at an air show at Kemble field, near Bristol, England. They had flown their newly complete Lancair across the pond to England and were planning on continuing to Germany. I was nearing the end of my 2003 around-the-world trip. We happened to be at the registration booth at the same time and struck up a conversation. Since then, we've met, talked, and emailed many times. They are planning several around-the-world trips and are building a new Lancair four-seater with custom designed fuel tanks.

Today we'd planned to meet in northern Florida, near their airpark home. I hadn't told them about my current plans, so this came as a surprise to them. They had lots of questions, input, ideas, and suggestions. We talked for several hours, then it was time to fly home.

I had in my mind to use a "distributed command center." Rather than having everyone in the same room, I thought of using three pilots living in different countries around the world. They'd have all the parameters, phone numbers, and email addresses, and each would be responsible for certain legs of the trip. I was thinking of asking Bill and Sue to handle the Pacific to Guam and the return leg across the Atlantic. I didn't discuss this with them during our meeting; but knew they were right for the job.

January 10, 2008 — PJ in Virginia

My oldest brother, Peter John, and I were clearing out Dad's house in Virginia when he asked a few questions and I started talking about my proposed adventure. I hadn't talked with family up to this point, but it was time to start explaining my objective.

He was a wealth of ideas and suggestions (to my surprise). He gave me his perspective as a vice president who had been solicited for donations during his working life. He tore apart my web site (as nicely as he could, but felt badly afterwards) and made strong recommendations for modifications. We talked one evening then off and on the next day. I returned home with a long list of improvements for promoting the trip and for the web site.

January 13, 2008 — KORL, Orlando Executive Airport

I've just finished meeting with friends from my EAA chapter in Orlando. I'd talked with Dave Berelsman in November, when Dad was dying and I needed to get away and get my mind on other things. We'd had breakfast and he'd given me lots of ideas. With the death and subsequent weeks passing, and the holidays, I'd done most of what he'd suggested, but needed to go to the next level. He'd recommended meeting with another EAA Chapter member, Chris.

I flew to Orlando Executive. The weather was terrible as a front was stalled just north of me in Ocala, but the forecast showed it lifting enough to get in with an instrument approach. With the 8am airport weather showing a higher ceiling, I set off. I was in fog but received a void time to depart from our private strip. After climbing through 2000 feet, I was on top of the clouds and in the bright sunshine, beautiful. ATC vectored me around to the runway 07 approach and down the glide slope I went. It was hazy but not solid overcast and I saw the runway and landed. It was less of an event than forecast.

Dave and wife, Lyn, were prepared with a "new and improved" executive summary of the project for Chris to read. I had the web site started and the route laid out. I had a picture of the Mooney

Dave, CarolAnn and Chris, the Orlando marketing team

with potential locations for decals for companies wishing to donate to ALS and become affiliated with the world-record attempt.

Chris had good contacts with local TV stations in the area and with Discovery Channel. He'd take the lead on making those contacts. We also discussed having a "command center." I'd been thinking of using a distributed network of pilot/friends around the world; however, having centralized communication, especially with the media, might be necessary. We'd give that more consideration.

I departed on a high. Showalter FBO waived the parking fee; thank you! And I have another long list of things to do. But, with help this time.

Several days later, I receive an email from Chris. One of his employees, a young man with twin four-year-old daughters has just been diagnosed with ALS. This is the typical profile, a male between 35 and 50 with a young family. He may choose to prolong his life by going on a respirator in a few years, so that he can see his children grow up. If not, he'll die when they are between seven and nine years old. That's why we are raising donations for ALS research, so these people, victims of ALS, can see their kids grow up.

January 15, 2008 — While on an Angel Flight

I was headed southeast at 6000 feet after taking off just before dawn. The sky was turning red through the high clouds off the coast ahead of me. The day was clear and I could see across Orlando to the Atlantic Ocean. My mind started wandering and I started smiling... I was looking forward to another adventure, to crossing that coastline and heading over the ocean. Well, not exactly the coastline ahead of me, but soon to cross the coast of California and head out again across the Pacific with a very specific goal. I was ready. Of course, it didn't help that I was reading *Chasing the Wind* in the evening. What an adventurer and inspiration Fossett was.

CHAPTER 2
STARTING THE FUNDRAISING

January 19, 2008 — Meeting with Lou, ALS-TDI

I was pumped when Lou of ALS-TDI left. We'd talked on the phone previously, and now he was in Orlando and had offered to meet in person. Peter John was with me for a few days, on his way to Key West, so he helped with the conversation. Lou had a friend who had died from ALS and that's how he got involved and started helping ALS-TDI with fundraising. Most of the employees are passionate about their job because they have known someone who has suffered from ALS. Lou loved the idea because it was different from any previous fundraising endeavor. The companies would donate to ALS to become affiliated with the world-record attempt and to have their logos on the plane and on our flight suits. Their donation made them a "good guy" to their customers and employees as they were donating to research, not to sponsoring the adventure. They couldn't lose. All we had to do was to figure out how to get to the right person in each company. We'd brainstormed giving levels, TV coverage, and what companies might be best for the "Title" position; i.e. the company that would donate a large sum to get their company name and logo associated with the event, web site, book, etc.

Several weeks later I had a phone conference with Lou, Molly, and Alicia, all from ALS-TDI. We pushed further with ideas and split up assignments. Our objective was to raise one million dollars for ALS research; mainly from companies becoming affiliated with this project by donating to ALS. I would put together a list of potential donors, at least the aviation related companies. Alicia would start on the logo and draft of a brochure.

February 12, 2008

Ahhh, taxes are done, for today; lay them aside and re-look tomorrow. Now I can concentrate on the trip planning, my favorite project. As it's been sitting in the back of my mind, I've been thinking about backup plans and contingencies. I think I'm going to plan an optimum route with a backup stop; and, calculate what the winds and gas situation need to be to continue or to move to plan B. This will make me feel better. As I watched the winds during November and December 2007, they were mostly as forecast, but infrequently unfavorable. I wanted to plan for that unfavorable eventuality.

The longest legs that will need contingency plans are across the Pacific, the Atlantic, and across Africa. I started working on Africa. From Djibouti to Mali is 2995 nautical miles or 21.4 hours direct, without considering winds or airways. Predominant winds are easterly at 20 to 30 knots, so conservatively we should be able to do the direct route in 18.6 hours. Now, consider that we'll have to fly airways and that Chad won't allow access directly from Sudan, so we'll have to fly further south. That makes the route 3117 nautical miles and 22.2 hrs before favorable winds or 19.4 hours with conservative winds. Our fuel exhaustion limits are 22 hours at 75% power and 24 hours at 65% power.

I look at an option to fly from India to Nairobi, Kenya and then to Mali. The raw numbers are 2798 nautical miles and 19.8 hours, but with airways we jump to 2898 nautical miles and 20.6 hours prior to tailwinds. This is doable without tailwinds, but more difficult if the winds aren't favorable. I saw that case only two times while I was watching the weather this past November and December. But, it could happen; what is our contingency plan for headwinds? I'll have to find a stopping point more central in Africa. The issue being that not all the countries are friendly and not all have avgas. One of my earlier choices had been to stop further east, in Niger instead of Mali; I'll have to go back to looking at options there.

In the Pacific and Atlantic, the options are more limited; if we can't make Guam, we'll have to divert to the Marshall Islands. If we can't make it across the Atlantic, we'll have to stop in the Caribbean,

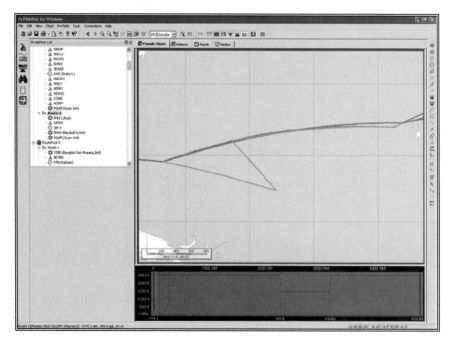

Planning tool: Upper right, Lihue, Hawaii. Center left, Guam.
Triangular line showing diversion point to Majuro, Marshall Islands,
if necessary.

Puerto Rico, or the US Virgin Islands. It's just a matter of doing the calculations ahead of time and setting the rules for the decision point. We don't want to be second guessing ourselves in the air.

Hawaii to Guam is 3217 nautical miles or about 21.3 hours before tailwinds. All data have shown me tailwinds from 20 to 40 knots. Taking a conservative 20 knots, our time would be 18.7 hours, very doable. But in case we get unlucky, at what point should we make our decision to divert to the Marshall Islands?

That's it for the evening; back to doing taxes in the morning; it's been a fun time working on the trip but the rest of life has to take over from dreaming.... Hopefully I'll have more time tomorrow evening.

February 14, 2008

After a good night's sleep and lots of thinking about the trip, I contacted two friends to start work on turn-around time in Thailand

and Guam. Might as well get the ground crew started. I've sent emails and can't wait to hear back from them. I also solved my Africa distance and winds problem. We fly right over Niamey, Niger. That was one of my original planned stops. That will be our plan B in case of headwinds. This will also eliminate the need to go further south to Kenya. Who knows what the political situation will be at the end of this year? Right now they have civil unrest after the election and thousands have been killed. I'm sure things will improve over the next ten months, however, it would mean more miles overall. Sticking with Djibouti and having a plan B in Niger is simpler.

OK, now back to the Pacific. Where's our decision point? We can actually fly beyond the Marshall Islands and if we have headwinds such that we won't make Guam, we'll have plenty of endurance to get back to the Islands. It's like two legs of a triangle: the first into the wind and the second with the wind. It'll take less time to get back to the Marshall Islands than to complete the leg to Guam. Again, I don't think this will be necessary, but it's best to have a contingency plan.

If we had headwinds and it looks like we won't make Guam by the middle of the leg, that's about ten hours of flying and it's only five hours to the Marshall Islands. The final decision must be made by 2100 miles into the leg at which point we'll have 1100 remaining to Guam and only 840 to the Marshall Islands.

I just received an email from a pilot in Hawaii. He'd found my web site and enjoyed reading about my 2003 trip. I've sent him an email to see if he knows anything about the airport in Lihue, on one of the western islands of Hawaii. Maybe we'll get some local help.

Feb 14th, 2008 — Afternoon, after baking a cake

I sent in my application for National Aeronautic Association (NAA) membership and a Sport License that is required to apply for a record attempt. Now we are really underway!

There are lots of rules and regulations; hopefully they won't be overbearing. At the same time the web site listed the companies supporting the NAA, some of which might be good sponsors for our record attempt. Can't get there without trying.

How to get those donations… that's pummeling my brain. We have to identify the potential companies, find a high-ranking manager, get access to that person, prepare the documentation, then make the pitch. Well, we'll start with Mooney next week. I have an invitation to a meeting with their public relations person in Ft. Lauderdale; that'll be my first test. Then I'll have more of an idea what to expect as we approach other companies.

February 19, 2008

The monthly Mooney pilots' lunch had been held at Ft. Lauderdale Executive airport several weeks ago. Usual crowd, nice time, good food, lots of Mooney talk. My "twin" Mooney was there, N221FC. Chuck and I had met several years ago, but we'd never got our planes together for a picture. When a few planes had left and there was time, I pulled my plane over next to Chuck's, found some people with cameras and asked them to take some pictures. They look wonderful together. The longer story is that our two planes are part of a group of four that were manufactured together in 1992/3 for a flight school in Fort Collins, Colorado; thus the FC at the end of the registration. Mine was the only one that went to Colorado and during my first world trip I actually received an email from a pilot who had flown in it when only 11 hours were on the Hobbs meter. I also received an email from the CEO running Mooney at the time; reflecting on the four identical Mooneys going through the factory.

Chuck and CarolAnn with N221FC and N220FC, identical Mooneys.

The flight school folded and my Mooney went to another flight school in Texas. The second of the group of four Mooneys, Chuck's, went to a private owner in California and he bought it in 2001 with only 1000 hours on the engine. Mine had 5300 at the time. We've heard of N223FC for sale in Texas and I talked with potential buyers in Utah but haven't seen the plane. We don't know what happened to the fourth. We were still happy to get ours together and have the pictures.

During the lunch a couple that I didn't know sat at our table and the woman, Cathy, started asking questions about my 2003 trip. She told her husband who I was then they introduced themselves; Fred and Cathy Ahles, President, VP, and owners of Premier Aircraft Sales, not only in Ft. Lauderdale, but also located in Orlando, Vero Beach, Atlanta, Raleigh, Richmond, Dallas, Houston, San Antonia, etc. Wow, I didn't realize who they were. So I continued answering questions about the trip and eventually someone asked about a future trip. I started explaining about the three-year-trip I was planning (so that I didn't talk about the upcoming Dash) and kept the timing pretty vague. They wanted to buy my first book, *Upon Silver Wings,* so after lunch I retrieved one from the Mooney and found Cathy so I could autograph it for both of them.

Cathy was thinking about how to support and promote my future trip and mentioned that folks from the Mooney factory would be visiting in a few weeks. Maybe I could stop by during their meetings and talk about my next adventure. Little did Cathy know what an opportunity she was offering.

During the interim, with ALS-TDI folks, we put together a package of information. The day arrived and I was all set to fly back down to Ft. Lauderdale Executive Airport. I was pretty calm, the weather was great with good tailwinds on the way down. A few miles out I started to get butterflies and wondered how this would go. I'd made copies of all the information for them, but I'd forgotten a copy for myself — losing my business training already. I decided to explain that we really weren't ready to go public, but wanted to take this opportunity to talk with Mooney, since they were here, and maybe they had ideas that could help this cause.

When the meeting started, it was obvious that Cathy had told them a little about my upcoming trip, and they'd thought about TV coverage during the departure, especially if it could happen during the upcoming NBAA, National Business Aviation Association, meeting in Orlando. Well, I had to stop them going in the wrong direction. So, I explained that we really weren't ready to go public, but that this was going to be a "world-record attempt." Their eyes really lit up. They started reading the information that I'd handed out. The conversation was constructive, productive, and very helpful to me. They each took items to work on and we parted with a positive commitment to have a news release at Sun 'N Fun, the spring air show at Lakeland, Florida.

During the flight home my mind was a whirlwind with lots of positive thoughts and feelings. So many ideas put forth, much bigger than mine. They have great contacts in different businesses. I'm fine on the technical and planning side, but this is a different ball game.

As I approach Ocala, the sun is a red ball going down into the smoky horizon to the west. There is smoke everywhere from fires. I'm looking forward to watching sunsets over the ocean; they'll come soon enough.

February 20, 2008

Heading out over the Gulf on another Angel Flight, I'm looking at the darker blue water as it merges with the lighter blue skyline. Why does that attract me so much? Guess I want to go there, to new places over the horizon. I understand why people want to live on the coast, looking out over the sea. You can lose yourself and your mind to dreams and possibilities. Well, our next possibility will be later this year, only seven months away. I know the time will pass quickly and be busy. Hopefully we'll meet all our objectives, raise one million dollars in donations for ALS research, break the world record, and have fun at the same time.

A change in the route "wakes" me from my reverie, but also reminds me that I need to meet and talk with the center controllers and understand routing across the Gulf and inbound from the Atlantic. Getting the first and last legs approved through ATC and knowing that we won't have any deviations, especially on the long final leg, could definitely impact the flight time and frustration level.

February 21, 2008

I fly my little homebuilt RANS down to Clearwater, just northwest of Tampa/St. Pete. A storm has blown through and the ceiling is fine, but it's a little bumpy and I set out early due to headwinds. I'm meeting another Angel Flight board member, Evan and his wife, Ronnie. I just joined the board six months ago and found Evan, with his marketing background, to be a fount of information and a great help. I disclosed my project to him after the last meeting in December and sent him some updates. This is our first meeting on details of the project.

He and especially Ronnie had many ideas as well as mentally putting together a game plan. Ronnie had raised money for hospitals, museums, and other not-for-profit organizations in the area and knew it could be done. She was positive and kept thinking of more ideas. I left inspired once again. But, also, maybe a little daunted; this was going to be a BIG job. I enjoy the planning and flying, but the fundraising, speaking with media, etc. isn't where my heart is. So, I was mentally mixed during the return trip; inspired by the trip and the potential but a little weighed down by the requirements that would be put on me over the next seven months.

February 22, 2008

It was time to put together a list of tasks, distribute it to all marketing volunteers, and figure out what's next.

Instead, I pulled out a chart of the Gulf and looked at the special use airspace over the western Gulf and the limited airways. I need to find an air traffic controller to talk with about the optimum way across. That's what I wanted to do. But, no, I'll get to the other job first!!

March 4-9, 2008 — Cape Town, South Africa
Earthrounders meeting

The Earthrounders are an informal group of pilots that get together every two to three years somewhere in the world. Their web site, www.earthrounders.com has lots of helpful information for long-distance pilots and potential Earthrounders and lists the people and planes that have circumnavigated the earth since the first one in 1929 (when German pilot Baron Koenig-Warthausen flew around the continents but shipped his plane over the oceans). American Wiley Post was the first to fly all the way around in 1933 setting a speed record of 15,000 miles in 18 days.

This year over 30 of us met in Cape Town, South Africa, for four days of roundtable discussions and tourist activities. Even during the bus rides, we were all swapping seats and sharing information with other pilots. It was a wonderful injection of memories of long-distance flying and reminders of the good and difficult aspects of global touring in your own small plane.

I had prepared a page of information about my planned trip and found the right time to open the subject to the other pilots. They were extremely helpful with thoughts, ideas and most importantly contacts in other countries. It was a great exchange, and I couldn't wait to return to my computer (back in the US) to check some optional countries and modify my route. Another pilot was headed down through Africa and brought out his charts which we sat around and everyone gave their input and experience. He also modified his trip (he had his laptop with him) that evening and was all smiles the next day as the input and new route worked out perfectly. Now I was even more impatient to return to my laptop and routing.

The final formal dinner was also the handover ceremony to the next host. Margi and Gerard Moss, living in Brazilia, received the Earthrounders' flag and are going to develop a program for our next meeting in Brazil in June 2010. We were all looking forward to it and many from the US and Europe plan to fly their planes there.

March 13, 2008

I arrived home at 8:30pm and turned on my laptop; jet lagged and tired, I couldn't wait any longer. I wasn't going to do it all, I just wanted to find out if a leg from Thailand to Oman and then to Khartoum and Bamako, Mali would be better than my current routing. It was!! The distances were more balanced, it skipped a stop in India, and reduced the long leg to Mali. Yeah, now I can go to bed.

March 18, 2008

Much time has been spent on marketing and web site development. Of course I had to fly my planes. They don't like to sit on the ground for too long and neither do I. The day after I returned from South Africa, I flew my RANS around the local lake and enjoyed the scenery. That evening I took my biplane for a spin and practiced my landings — they still need work. On the Friday I was headed to an Angel Flight board meeting, which meant that my Mooney would be getting its workout. Once that was all finished I turned to the serious routing issues.

The overall legs now looked good. The major remaining issues are:

- Is there avgas in Guam?
- Who can do weather forecasting (the movement of pressure systems over the Pacific to forecast the tailwinds for departure)?
- A complete breakdown of each leg into the airway routes and review country over-flight requirements.
- The two longest legs, Hawaii to Guam and Cape Verde to Florida didn't bother me too much; but I wanted to finalize the alternate stops in case of headwinds.

April 4, 2008

What a LOW. Two weeks ago Lou and I had talked with Mooney about donating to ALS to become a sponsor affiliated with this project. This had been a follow-up to our conversation in Fort Lauderdale in February. Cyndi Roth, Director of Marketing and Communications, had said that Mooney was looking at non-financial help and were still discussing a budget number if possible. They were to follow-up this week, but I hadn't received any calls or emails. They had planned a press release at Sun 'N Fun (SNF) to announce our world-record attempt trip along with other Mooney business. I need to know those details as well as their sponsorship level. I also had to finish the website and get it up to my web host in Virginia. I was listing the donors/sponsors on a "Thank you" page on the site. I'd already listed Mooney along with several other companies as I designed the page. I'd already bought Mooney patches to put on our flight suits.

Well, Cyndi finally returned my call. Mooney wasn't going to be able to donate to ALS. I was heartbroken. I hadn't counted on a lot, but at least a small donation to recognize the coverage they would be receiving from the trip and the media. I said that we wouldn't be going ahead with the press release. Cyndi said that she understood.

I'd already received rejections from Virgin Atlantic, Breitling, and Avemco. This fundraising wasn't my cup of tea. Salesmen have the right makeup to keep on going after each rejection. I was feeling low and depressed.

Two more days to get everything finished before SNF. I get the web site as finished as it's going to be. I eliminate the "Thank you" page and get the rest sent off to my web host, Wanda, in Virginia. With Ronnie and the ALS support staff, we'd spent much time preparing, editing and had finally completed a brochure on the project. They had been printed and Lou would be bringing them down to SNF.

Sunday, the day before departure to Lakeland, I'm throwing my camping gear in the car and forget the tarp pegs. I pack everything I think I need (without the usual thought process) and end up with only one pair of jeans. And, believe it or not, I leave the piece of paper with my daily itinerary and people to contact on my desk. I start realizing all these oversights as I'm driving down on Monday morning. Let's hope it doesn't rain as I won't have the extra protection from the tarp. Let's hope there isn't a cold spell during the week as I'll freeze. And, luckily a neighbor is driving down on

Tuesday and he can bring my itinerary with him. Looking back on all these mistakes, I know this isn't my usual process and I've been a little overloaded these past two weeks.

April 7-13, 2008 — Sun 'N Fun, Lakeland, FL

Many in our EAA chapter go down early to set up. We work/volunteer in General Aviation (GA) Parking. We marshal the planes from where they taxi off the runway to their parking or camping locations. Most of the volunteer group is seasoned and know what needs to be done. This year is different. We've had rain for three days. The parking areas are lakes. The camping area on the west end of the field is closed. We're putting campers in the parking area (although there are no facilities or showers). The vintage parking can't take their normal number of planes so they end up in GA parking also. The hardtop area, usually reserved for heavy twins, is a mish-mash of homebuilts, twins, single engine planes, and people camping on the grass by their plane on the hard top. Finally, it's obvious that parking will have to be closed to inbound traffic on the Tuesday morning. Until the grass dries out and the planes get moved to their normal locations, this is going to be a maze.

Monday evening I head to Tampa International to pick up Carol. We have a hotel halfway between Tampa and Lakeland for ease of travel and because everything in Lakeland is booked. We spend the evening catching up and talking about the trip. Carol has some GREAT ideas for fundraising from her racing days. Ask people to sponsor/donate a mile of the route and more of a donation for their name attached to a stop point. I fall asleep thinking that if people donated just $10 per mile that would mean $200,000 for ALS. I kept recalculating the number in my head. Wow, this was BIG. Wow, what a great idea. Wow, this could work.

Carol and I talked on the way to SNF; we were to meet Lou and Ronnie at the registration area. I told her about my calculations while falling asleep. She agreed, it had worked for her races and it could work for ALS donations. Paul, a friend from Texas called Carol. She talked with him about the $10/mile donation and he donated $100. Yep, this was going to work.

We met Lou and Ronnie after they had slogged through the mud in the car parking area and had it squishing between their toes. Later that week Sun 'N Fun would be called "Mud 'N Fun" by the media. We had to watch where we walked. But we went to the Mooney booth and met Dennis Ferguson, President, and Cyndi Roth with whom we'd been communicating about sponsorship. Premier Aircraft Sales, the number one Mooney dealer, were there and I introduced Lou, Ronnie and Carol to Fred Ahles, the president and Cathy, his wife and Senior VP of Marketing and Business Development. Cathy gave me a hard copy of the press release that Fred was going to make. Wow, we were blown away. What a wonderful statement:

> Hi. I'm Fred Ahles of Premier Aircraft Sales in Fort Lauderdale. We're the Mooney dealer for the Southeast United States.
>
> When I founded Premier five years ago, it was with a deep conviction that those of us in the aviation community should use the resources available to us to help others in need. Since that time, our company has been involved in a number of social initiatives like building homes in Haiti and Jamaica and running a bone marrow drive for a child with leukemia.
>
> Today I want to tell you about a remarkable aviator who shares this deep belief that we should give back to the community.
>
> CarolAnn Garratt embodies the typical "Mooniac." She has the heart of an adventuress and the soul of missionary. And this year, she has a very special mission in mind.
>
> You see, her mother died of ALS, or Lou Gehrig's Disease. Since that time CarolAnn has dedicated herself to raising money for research to find a cure for this terrible disease.
>
> ALS is a degenerative disease that attacks motor neurons in the brain and spinal cord. When the neurons can no longer send impulses to the muscles due to ALS, they begin to waste away, causing increased muscle weakness, loss of mobility and, eventually, death.
>
> CarolAnn and her associate, Carol Foy, will attempt to set a world record this fall by flying around the world in 7 days. Their chances are good. A couple years ago she

Carol and CarolAnn at the Mooney booth at Sun 'N Fun

flew her Mooney around the world in about seven months, so she has some experience with a flight of this magnitude.

They need our help. CarolAnn and Carol are paying 100% of the expenses for this adventure, but they need individual and corporate sponsors to help move them toward their goal of raising $1 million for the ALS Therapy Development Institute.

I'd like to ask everyone in this room to help us spread the word about her Dash for the Cure. If she's going to raise $1 million, she needs our help in the form of visibility for her effort and direct contributions to the cause. Every contribution, no matter how large or how small, will move her one step closer to her goal. Please make this a personal priority. CarolAnn is here today and I'm sure she'd be glad to answer any questions you might have.

Thanks.

It went extremely well. We couldn't thank them enough. What a start to SNF. We talked with several magazine writers afterwards as well as some Mooniacs who had recognized me from presentations at their flying clubs.

OK, now it's time to get to work. In order to start the fundraising, we were going to speak with the aviation-related companies who have booths in the four hangars at SNF. We split up with Lou and me hitting hangars C&D and Carol and Ronnie going to the vendors in hangars A & B. It wasn't long before a phone call got us together again to discuss details on approach and how things were going. Most vendors took the information and said they'd run it by management after SNF. Some were offering products. That

CarolAnn and Carol giving a presentation at the Sun 'N Fun museum.

wasn't the objective; we are paying for the adventure, we're looking for donations. Split up and keep going. Lou and I covered all the vendors in hangar C and just started on D when the phone rang.

Back together again, product was what we are going to get; we'll need to find a way, probably a raffle, to exchange products for donations.

After a long day Ronnie and Lou headed home and Carol and I hit a few more vendors before Carol headed back to the hotel and I headed to the flight line to help with departures and arrivals (my volunteer job at SNF and AirVenture in Oshkosh, Wisconsin).

April 9, 2008

Wednesday morning I have to head to the museum for the Author's Corner and a presentation. Carol joins me at the end of the presentation to explain about our upcoming adventure. The crowd asks lots of questions and genuinely seems excited to hear the news.

Susan Genett's Real Weather, "Your Custom Forecast Resource," had been Carol's weather forecaster for her last few races. She'd received weather options that helped her make decisions that supported the win in 2006. So, we had a phone conference planned. Susan didn't have much information on our planned trip and didn't know, but had suspected, that it was a world-record attempt. We both had questions for Susan.

After learning that Susan had supported Richard Branson's balloon flights and races as well as a number of sailing races, I was pleased with her background. During our conversation, Carol asked if December was a good time to make the flight. Susan's response pleased me enormously. She said that it was the best time for this type of flight with cool temperatures and pressure systems further north. In the spring they descend southward. I hadn't thought about asking that question but was pleased to have my analysis confirmed by an expert. Overall it was a good conversation and we all decided to take it to the next level. Susan would work up an estimate to support our flight and I'd plan to meet her in Rhode Island during my next trip to Boston in early May.

April 10-13, 2008

I dropped Carol off at Tampa. She was not looking forward to the flight home. American Airlines had announced hundreds of flight cancellations due to maintenance issues. Carol called me while I was driving to SNF. It'd take all day, but she'd get home. She hadn't flown her Mooney to SNF due to running a half-marathon in New York just before SNF. A Mooney flight home would be MUCH quicker than this day of three airline flights and airport waiting time. But, at least she'd make it home.

The last three days I split my time between the Author's Corner, making presentations in the museum, talking with vendors in the hangars, and directing traffic on the taxiways. Oh yes, I did have a beer or wine in the evenings with friends on the flight line. They were sleeping in campers on real beds; I was in a pup tent on the ground in a sleeping bag. It was a sunny, warm, dry week. Unfortunately a storm was coming through on Sunday. We spent the morning on the flight line as usual. Business was quiet as it was the last day. We had more departures than arrivals. With the breeze, our tents dried quickly from the dew and we took turns going in and packing everything up before the storm hit. My shift ended and I was replaced just before the rain started.

April 14, 2008

I kept waking up thinking of everything I have to do today... after Sun 'N Fun in Lakeland, Florida where we met a gazillion potential donors and came up with lots of new ideas, I have SO much to do. As I was driving home yesterday evening, I was writing notes on the box next to me to list everything, especially the urgent items that need to get done today.

I've already sent an email to Elissa at EAA about our idea to do a "24-hour simulation" at AirVenture. Wow, that would be a great fundraising event if they'll let us do it. We'd essentially sit in the plane most of the time, but get out to simulate refueling at stops and do a long 17-hour leg overnight. It'll also be a good test for Carol and me to see what we haven't thought of or what else we might need to do for creature comforts.

I received new information about tanking and the FAA over-gross requirements, so I put a call into the FAA this morning. I called the National Aeronautics Association, NAA, to get more information on the sanction needed for a World Record attempt.

I also learned that Globe Aero Ltd, the company that did my tanking for my 2003 trip is going to be sold by the end of the month. I need to speak with Phil and try to buy several items that I used on my 2003 trip.

That's the end of the urgent list, but the follow-up from Sun 'N Fun contacts will take all week. Better get to work. Wow, this is coming together. I'm feeling good... maybe even great, definitely energized. Hope there aren't too many "lows" along the way as some rejections come in and as some of our plans require tweaking and modifications.

Look at all those little pieces of paper... I tend to write down notes on anything I can find, and I've LOTS of notes from the past week. OK, time to make one list of everything.

April 15, 2008 — Ronnie managing expectations

I spent all day updating our spreadsheet of potential donors and media and getting separate thoughts out to the ALS team, especially updating the brochure and an analysis of our potential donations. Although positive, it's not outstanding.

I got an unexpected call from Ronnie. I thought we were going to discuss next steps but she was more interested in managing my expectations. I'd never had someone worry about me before, so this was interesting! She knew from the emails that I'd reached the conclusion that without big sponsors we weren't going to reach the million-dollar mark. She wanted to be sure I was OK. Which I was/am. But I'm still pushing. Without media and TV coverage we won't get the big sponsors. We'll end up at half a million in donations for ALS research. Not bad, but not what we are striving for.

April 17, 2008

Well, another big step forward today — the diaper leaked! I thought I'd try it before my eight-hour trip to Boston in two weeks. So, after two cups of coffee, around 9am, I put on the diaper and the red flight suit and sat down to work. Nothing. So I got a cup of coffee around 10am. Nothing, I kept on working. I started feeling uncomfortable, but no pee.

I started getting frustrated, unable to work and unable to pee. Around noon I got a glass of water and sat on the sofa to read a magazine. Actually the chair at my desk is pretty hard and the diaper was uncomfortable; a lesson already for the plane. I thought the sofa, being softer, would be better and it was. Still no pee. I got another glass of water and kept reading. I peed a little, but not much. Finally I moved back to my desk and back to work. Then it came. It was an interesting feeling, not like peeing as there was pressure from the diaper, not a free flow. So, I kept peeing. Then I saw liquid on the flight suit, oh NO, it was leaking. I let it soak into the flight suit and walked gingerly to the bathroom, taking the suit off in the laundry on the way. The diaper looked pretty full. At least at the front, not at the back.

I think I need to talk with a diaper specialist to understand how these things work. I'd drunk a lot of water and, once it started, peed quite a bit very quickly. I wonder how many quarts this thing holds. Maybe I'll try dumping water in it, like the TV commercials. Better try it again on the ground before flying in the Mooney. Not today, that's enough.

April 23, 2008

I've been working on a spreadsheet with times and dates to see when the best time of day would be to start and when we would arrive at each stop. Our parameters are to fly over the Rocky Mountains during daylight and try to arrive at foreign airports during their hours of operation.

Although it's possible to estimate speeds and wind, I tend to be on the conservative side and arrive early when I fly to places. That's not going to work for this seven-day trip. I am forcing myself to be more accurate with estimates and winds. I'll run it by Carol when I get a plan that I'm happy with. She'll add the critical element that we need as well as having other ideas.

Right now I've estimated a four-hour stop in Thailand because I need to do an oil change there as well as inspect and sign off two Aircraft Directives. Also, we'll have friends meeting us there, so this should be an "easy" stop. Based on timing, we'd be arriving at Salalah, Oman, the stop after Thailand, too early in the morning, so we could stay longer in Thailand and maybe get a shower and rest. Another option is to take a rest in Guam as we'll have already flown two nights before arriving there. It would be three nights before Thailand, so Guam would be "safer" from a fatigue point of view. Right now we don't have a contact in Guam. We'll have to make that a priority. Take maybe six to eight hours rest in Guam and a two- to three-hour stop in Thailand.

When looking at the rest of the trip, the arrivals fall into place during normal business hours. When looking more closely I realize that it puts us flying over Africa during the night and over the Atlantic Ocean during the night. Gulp, is that what we want? It would be nice to split it up but that makes for nighttime arrivals in foreign countries. I don't think that's what we need either. Hmmm, it'll be smoother at night. Not as much air traffic to worry about nor Air Traffic Control issues. This might work out.

April 24, 2008

I thought about it a week ago, it's the anniversary of my mother's death from ALS. I didn't think it would be as memorable after six years, but it is. It started with an email from Chuck, who does ALS' website and was offering to help with mine. We had exchanged emails to get together by phone; he asked if I meant this Thursday the 24th, or the following Thursday. Yep, it's today. Six years ago today, I was in Orlando for some doctors appointments. Dad left the message on my answering machine. I called my brothers to let them know the news. I flew up to Virginia the following morning and picked up a brother in Atlanta along the way. It was a difficult time.

Today, I received a letter and donation from a friend, with a newspaper clipping about an ALS patient going by wheelchair from Florida to Washington, DC to raise awareness of ALS in veterans.

They, veterans, are being diagnosed with ALS at twice the rate of the normal population. He wants the government to start funding research. We do too!!

The chairman of ALS-TDI has ALS also. He, Augie Nieto, was diagnosed in 2005. I'll meet him next week in Cambridge, Massachusetts, and apparently he's in a wheelchair with little ability to move and his speech is not always understandable. We HAVE to raise this money. It's a horrible disease affecting 30,000 people in the US with 5,000 dying every year and 5,000 new cases being diagnosed. OK, off my soapbox and back to work.

Sunday April 27, 2008

Wow, some things are just meant to be; it's amazing the coincidences that happen. Some would say that there are no coincidences; anyway, it happened again.

Lou sent me an email to contact a woman who was a new ALS Ambassador who might be able to help with the project. Well, I was a little miffed. I'm already working 12 hours a day, and he's passing this on to me. He could figure out how she could help and get her going. Anyway, I called Pat. What a conversation; almost an hour of brainstorming how we could work together.

The biggest coincidence is that we're working on major sponsors and Budweiser is on the list. A friend of mine has a friend who knows Augie Busch and has accepted to make a pitch for our cause, ALS. I was telling Pat about this and her husband is a close friend of Augie Busch's number one man. Amazing. We can work this from both sides. They would be a terrific Title Sponsor.

Then we moved on to how to work together. It would seem that if we could align our fundraising with Baldrige best practices it would lead to a more lucrative, for ALS, speaking tour after the flight. I've already committed two years of speaking and book selling, just as I did after the first flight. If we can ratchet up the level of speaking engagements and hit companies' conventions, they would donate big dollars to ALS. It would also be a benefit to major sponsors. Pat is thinking BIG and has great ideas. This could be even bigger than I'd imagined.

April 30, 2008, Flight to Boston

This was planned to be a seven-hour, non-stop flight. I wanted to simulate a long leg on our flight, so I donned my diaper and red flight suit. I didn't have any coffee but took one "no-doze" tablet to give my body the caffeine it needs to avoid a "caffeine headache." I'd used these tablets before on long hikes and know that they work fine.

It really felt awkward walking in "it" (the diaper) as I was getting the plane loaded. But, I really won't have too much walking during the real flight. Let's hope anyway. Everything went well for the first few hours. Actually, it was easier sitting in the plane than trying to work at my desk. I know that I'll have to "go" eventually, but no rush. During the test, I was impatient and wanted to get it over with. It'll come in time.

I feel a little pressure, not too much, too little to release, but slightly uncomfortable. At 10am, after three hours of flying, I have some food. It's better for me to eat on a time schedule and to limit my intake. I eat half an apple and half a Pop-Tart. OK, now you know my weakness. I enjoy a Pop-tart a day. I also stretched; we're going to need to do this, so I might as well start getting into good habits.

Six hours into the flight and I still haven't peed. I can feel more pressure. I try easing myself off the seat and supporting my weight on my arms to release the pressure and "go." It doesn't work. As I head in over land the turbulence increases and I'm bounced around. This should help I think, but no improvement. Finally I land after seven hours of flying and no peeing. It was very uncomfortable at the end, but it's very difficult to release into a diaper. Oh well, I'll drink coffee before the return flight, then I'll have to go.

May 1, 2008, ALS-TDI

We had a meeting scheduled with Dave McKanna, VP Development, prior to meeting Augie Nieto, Chairman. Dave gave us some information on Augie, most interestingly, he has received a diaphragm pacemaker and is breathing on his own, even in this late stage of ALS. He could keep going for a long time, especially with his energy level. Dave looked up as Augie came across the lobby.

As he wheeled toward us in his chair, I recognized his face from the picture in his book. A firm, fit, middle-aged man, in a wheelchair, with his body failing him. I understood that he could barely move his hands enough to activate the joystick on the wheelchair.

We stood up as a group and walked towards him. I put my hand on his as I introduced myself and Ronnie. After we all sat down, I launched into my short summary of my project as we only had 15 minutes of Augie's time. After my part, Ronnie started explaining what we needed, his contacts with major sponsors and media introductions. Then Augie spoke. His speech is slurred due to ALS. Many words we could understand, but some were difficult. His wife, Lynne, repeated for us immediately. The conversation flowed well. Augie had some ideas and contacts for sponsorships. One was Virgin Atlantic; I'd been rejected twice by them. Augie knew Sir Richard Branson. We supplied the event — he, Augie, could get some big sponsors. He asked about the flight. That was easy for me to describe, I knew the details intimately and started explaining. Augie was impressed, but not half as impressed as I was of him.

There was a tender moment. Augie started speaking with me directly while Ronnie, Dave and Lynne spoke. Unfortunately, I couldn't understand all his words and Lynne helped. He said "you know what I'm going through" with his eyes piercing though mine. I couldn't answer as tears welled up in my eyes. I covered his hand with mine. Yes, I knew what he was going through, my mother had gone through the same steps as the disease progressed. It hurt to think of her as I looked at him. There's only one end. I don't remember the words that stumbled out, but finally we got on to a safer subject and I was able to talk again. When I looked at the others, it was obvious that they had been moved also. Later, Dave said that he, Augie, had had the whole board moved to tears the previous day. What a powerful man.

With very limited movement, he types 50 words a minute with his feet as he's writing a new book and starting a new company to design equipment for handicapped people, using video gaming technology developed in California. In all my years working and meeting top people in companies and CEOs, I've never been so compelled or awed by anyone as I was by Augie. It was an amazing 20 minutes that we shared.

It was also enormously productive. Augie had agreed to approach two companies as major sponsors for our event. He also accepted to make contact with the *Today* show people who had interviewed him on two previous occasions. Dave, Ronnie and I talked for a while to solidify our actions, then we departed.

All I could think was the more I give, the more I receive in return. Not only had we met our objectives, we'd had an inspiring morning. We were all moved to do more, be more, raise more.

After a busy day at the ALS-TDI facility and two presentations to EAA Chapter 106 members I finally departed on Saturday afternoon. The first leg was a very short flight to Providence, Rhode Island, to meet a potential weather person for our trip, then a three-and-a-half-hour leg to Virginia to spend the rest of the weekend with Peter John. I found it funny when the ground controller at Providence commented on my "long" trip to Virginia. I had to correct him and told him that I'd had a non-stop seven-hour trip from Florida two days earlier. If he thought this was long, he'd have trouble accepting sixteen-hour legs. No sense trying to explain that over the radio.

We'd become closer over the past two years, Peter John and I, since the untimely death of a brother and while taking care of our dad. We'd seen more of each other this past year than in the last 10 years combined. We'd also spent much time discussing my trip and fundraising. He was a fount of information. I enjoy our time together as we share more with each other.

He had contacts in the energy industry; he'd made a presentation to them earlier in the year about my trip and sponsorship, but they commented that they only donated locally, not nationally. Their focus is their regional population, very understandable. PJ thought that if we could prove that ALS existed in their area, maybe they could donate. So, another fundraising prong was needed. I'd talk with Dave about that next week.

After a fun day sailing and an evening talking, it was time to depart the next morning. This time I'd have coffee. I was bound to pee on this three-and-a-half-hour flight. I donned my diaper and red flight suit.

After departure, it felt uncomfortable right from the start. This would be the leg where I'd test the diaper. Two hours later I still hadn't peed. This was frustrating. The pressure from sitting in the diaper stopped any release. The pressure in the bladder was terrible. Again I tried lifting my weight off the seat. This time it worked a little. Some pee was finally released; but the pressure was still there, the bladder wasn't empty. Well, it wasn't uncomfortable sitting in "it." Nothing different at all. I finally landed at home and hadn't had a good pee. I ran into the bathroom, took off the diaper and finally peed what must have been gallons — OK, I exaggerate — but it was a *lot*. The diaper was not going to work. I'd talk with my mechanic about putting in a relief tube, like guys use. We have flight suits with zippers from the bottom. We could sit on one leg to get the height needed, put the Lady Jane adapter, connected to a tube, in the correct position, and let go. That would have to be better.

OK, one more trip coming up at the end of May to Minneapolis. That'd be my next test one way or the other.

CHAPTER 3
NEXT LEVEL OF DETAILED PLANNING

May 7, 2008

 I don't often feel low, but I'm not having a good day. I heard from a pilot friend who's headed for the Seychelles. I emailed him my contacts there and asked for some information on Salalah, Oman, when he gets there. He said that they don't have avgas there; which is what I thought and had confirmed from some Internet websites. But, since they'd planned on stopping there, I thought they had more current information. It turns out they've had a barrel of avgas shipped there. So, Muscat may be our stop. I was hoping to stop at a smaller airport with less bureaucracy. I've asked Flemming to judge the two airports and advise his thoughts after passing through Oman. We could ship the avgas to Salalah and still stop there if it's much easier for getting in and out quickly.

That set me thinking more about Khartoum, Sudan. They don't have avgas either, but I have a contact who could get fuel there. Wouldn't it be simpler and easier just to stop in Djibouti, where they have avgas and are pretty easy for customs paperwork? I've been there before, they speak French, it would be a relatively quick stop. The problem is that it's too long a leg from Djibouti to Bamako, Mali if we don't have good tailwinds. We can't be absolutely sure of making Mali and would have to have an alternate stop in Naimey, Niger. I took out my Lonely Planet Guide and re-read about Niger.

Then I remembered an Earthrounder pilot that I'd met in Switzerland, Reto Godly. He often flies to Libya and might have stopped in Niger on his return from South America in 2006. I found his website; yep, he'd stopped there, not in Naimey, but he'd have some information. I've emailed him my questions. Now I feel better and can get back to other things.

May 16, 2008

Fred from Universal Weather called me this afternoon. Their company has supported numerous world-record attempts in the past and he'll take my information and "run it up the flagpole" to see if they'll support our cause. Wow, this could be BIG. I told him about our latest changes in itinerary and we chatted a little about Barrington Irving's trip last year (youngest pilot and first African American to fly solo around the world). They had supported his trip.

After hanging up, I compiled an email with all information and details we'd planned so far and sent it off. I hope they accept to work with us. It could be a tremendous help in some of the difficult countries.

This contact actually came from one of my presentations in Boston several weeks ago. I met Ray prior to my talk, and told him about my upcoming trip. He told me that he works for Universal Weather and they support trips like this. He pulled out his Blackberry and showed me updates on avgas availability in Nice, France. They'd just run out that week. He says they get updates all the time and could help with my trip. We'd emailed after my return and he called to tell me that several people from the main facility in Houston would call. Well, Friday afternoon, 5pm, they called. What a way to end the week. This would really help a lot. Now, I keep my fingers crossed that they will say yes next week.

May 20, 2008

It was today in 1927 that Charles Lindbergh started out on his non-stop trip across the Atlantic Ocean. I would NEVER have been an aviation pioneer such as Lindbergh or Wiley Post or even Geraldine Mock, the first woman to fly around the world in 1964. They did amazing long distance flying without today's benefits of satellite weather and GPS. I'm happy to do the long flights that I do, but with the safety net of improved communication and weather information. Lindbergh was out of communication with the world for 30 hours. On this trip I'll have a satellite phone as well as HF radio, which I had on my last trip.

However, some days when I'm working on weight and equipment we're going to need, I feel like Lindbergh. I feel like trimming the edges of the charts, dropping five pounds off my weight, taking the carpet off the floorboards, and getting the weight down as much as possible so that we can take on more avgas.

May 22, 2008

I'm on my way to Minneapolis for a niece's wedding. I have lots of tests lined up for this seven-and-a-half-hour flight: satellite phone, pee bottle, HSI, and Gami injectors. This is going to be a busy trip.

I take off just before 7am. What a beautiful, smooth morning. I planned on a low cruise altitude, to stay below headwinds as much as possible. After getting everything set and obtaining my clearance from Jacksonville approach, I was ready for my first satellite phone contact. I'd emailed Norm, my Mooney pilot friend from Thailand, who'd sold me his satellite phone (after completing his trip around the world in his Mooney). We'd set up this call for 8am, 7pm his time. I asked Jax center if I could go off frequency for a few minutes. They approved. I'd already done all the wiring, routing the headset through the sat phone intercom box, so I just plugged in the phone and dialed. In no time Norm said, "Hello" and we had a conversation. Well, it actually took me a little bit to figure out the knobs. I had to turn the volume up and the squelch down, then it worked. Norm had static on his end when no one spoke, I had good reception. We decided to do another test in an hour.

I gotta say, it's a LOT more comfortable NOT sitting in a diaper. Let's hope the new bottle works. This will be a test to see if a relief tube is usable in a relatively comfortable position. To be determined later in the flight. Right now I'm enjoying the seat. Actually, it's not my normal seat, it's the right seat moved into the left position. My seat is out and on its way to Oregon Aero for an upholster job. I chose to keep the same blue corduroy covers, but buy new, super duper cushions supporting correct posture. I really didn't have any trouble during my first trip in 2003, but this was going to be seven days, practically non-stop as far as sitting goes. So, I wanted a little insurance and comfort.

I was paying attention to Air Traffic Control (ATC) who was giving me an amendment to my clearance around Atlanta, which I copied down and repeated back. After that, I started executing the HSI tests that I'd been given. I had to un-slave the HSI and monitor the precession of the instrument. So, I did the checks and wrote down the heading changes relative to the compass direction. That's two tests down.

I called Norm again but this second contact had very poor reception on both ends. We didn't talk much and rescheduled one hour hence. That would put me north of Atlanta and probably higher, 6000 feet, not that altitude should have any impact on satellite phone reception.

I decided to try the pee bottle. The idea this trip was to sit on my right leg, with my foot under my butt to give me enough vertical elevation to slip a more flexible pee bottle into my flight suit (similar to using a relief tube). The position felt OK, I just didn't have to pee.... Will try again later. But, the important part was that the position felt that it would be doable with a relief tube.

I called Norm again. What a beautiful connection. It was like we were next to each other. The reception was clear, like talking on a land line, not a cell phone. We both felt good about the tests, confirmed that we'd be meeting in July in Oshkosh, and said our goodbyes.

On to the Gami tests. I had the sheet and charts out. We were past Nashville so the flying and ATC should be quiet for a while. Just as I was starting the test, the HSI went out again. I flew manually and noted the instrument behavior again. I slaved and unslaved the unit and put it back on autopilot. I wrote everything down to pass on to the avionics people. Then I went back to the Gami test.

Then a thought came to me. Everything could work great, or I could overcome some failures, BUT if the transponder went out, I wouldn't be allowed to continue the flight. I couldn't fly IFR and countries wouldn't accept my flying in their airspace without a transponder code. I'd have to put that on the list for redundancy; probably borrow someone else's transponder for the week. I'd have to test it ahead of time and get it approved for my plane. But, that's a little price to pay to be able to continue with the flight.

I think it's time, so I try to pee again...no go. It's difficult to "let go." But, again, the position feels OK. I'll check in to installing a relief tube when I return.

Well, this test flight has been going OK. I'm north of Peoria, Illinois and there are windmills everywhere. I start counting, there are over 100 of them. It looks like more are being installed. I wonder what percentage of power they provide. Usually I see them on hill tops, all in a line along the ridge. Here they are all over the place, in a patchwork. It must be windy down there most of the time. Fascinating.

The remainder of the flight and the flight home went well. Oh yes, the wedding went well also! All the best to my niece Devon and her new husband, Phil.

May 26, 2008

Back to work in the office the following week; I was still uncomfortable with Africa. I heard from my Swiss Earthrounder friend who confirmed that Niamey was not a good place to stop. I started looking north to Tunisia. That's a good country, tourist-friendly. Let's check distances. Wow, looks good. I emailed Reto again; he knew this part of Africa. I reconfirmed distances and started modifying our routing. Oman to Tunisia to Cape Verde. That looked better and felt safer. We'd have to fly over Saudi Arabia, but I'd received good reports from fellow pilots. They have been giving overflight permits and several friends were headed there. I'd get a first-hand account pretty soon.

May 29, 2008

We started the annual inspection on the Mooney today. Well, actually we'd started it earlier in the week, then spent that day tearing the engine apart to get all the major accessories out to companies for overhaul. They would be the long lead time items.

Today we started the body and engine inspection. During the day we did a lot of "what if's" and looking into overhauling more components or thinking of backup plans if something failed during the flight. The "we" is me and my aircraft mechanic with inspection authorization (A&P with IA), Art, who has worked on my Mooney for the past four years, including doing the engine installation after its overhaul in 2005.

After considering several issues, we decided to bring Wes Dale, the former Mooney service manager, now working for Premier Aircraft in Ft. Lauderdale, Florida, into the picture. I called him with our current question, the flap motor, but also gave him information on what we were doing and asked for more ideas. He listed a few issues to look into, then asked for a list of what was underway, so that he could give it more consideration.

Later in the day we started working out the hours on an instrument that had been replaced in 2001. I called the manufacturer and an overhaul shop. It seems we were running on "borrowed time" as he put it. So that went on the list for extraction and was shipped to the overhaul shop.

At the end of the day, the price of the annual inspection and repairs had increased significantly, but also the chance of success without failures en route had been improved. I felt that we were getting into the necessary details and would yet uncover a few more items, but it would pay off in the long run.

The annual inspection had been scheduled for June so that we could get all new or overhauled components onto the Mooney, then put another 100 hours on the equipment prior to the world flight. That should uncover any "infant mortality" or early failures. We would do another inspection after 100 hours and just before the world flight. We also planned to change the tires, brakes, tank O-rings, and any other components about 20 hours before the flight. This should ensure 140 flight hours without mechanical interruption during our world-record attempt.

June 2, 2008 — Lots of help

The guys and gals from Universal Weather and Aviation, Inc have been exchanging emails with me. It's looking good to get their help; and what a GREAT help they will be. Carol had read about them in *Professional Pilot* magazine. They do permits and weather for corporate planes traveling all over the world. They have tons of experience and will be a great asset during our trip.

Then there's the Michelin guy, Keat. He's looking into eight-ply tires. With the extra weight on taxi and takeoff, Art thought maybe eight-ply would be safer than the normal six-ply. Keat is doing the calculations. Actually, he had me doing lots of calculations to figure out the maximum weight on each wheel in normal and over gross conditions. From that, he'll make his recommendation.

One of the overhaul shops called. The alternator is not repairable. He explained about the problems and made a recommendation, which I accepted. He certainly sounded like he knew his products. Then the mechanic overhauling the fuel boost pump got on the line. That was going well; he explained what he'd changed and why. After 15 years, it needed an overhaul. Well, I'm now good for another 10 to 15 years (at least on that component).

The Mooney inspection is complete; nothing surprising. I've lubricated all the rod ends and greased all the zerks. After "BoShielding" (corrosion protection for those of us in southern, humid conditions) the interiors of the wings and fuselage, I reinstalled all the inspection ports. Now we just have to wait for the components to return. I can start by putting the magnetos, vacuum pump, and filter on, since those are new components that I already have on hand. By next week, we'll have the rest and can put it all back together again.

June 9, 2008

While waiting for components to be overhauled and returned, I get back to fundraising and flight planning. I'd modified the route over Africa to head north to Tunisia, then Cape Verde and across the Atlantic. The distances looked good until I referenced the wind charts I'd downloaded last December. I started rechecking all legs with the wind charts and distances. Everything looked good, actually VERY good, until Tunisia. There wasn't a day without winds blowing 20 to 30 knots from the west. We'd never make it there. No way; out of the question. Actually, just going further north to Muscat instead of Salalah introduced some slight headwinds. The further south we stayed the better the easterly tailwinds. If we try to head north we'd lose out to headwinds.

Now, back to the drawing board: how to get across Africa, staying further south? I checked the distance from Djibouti to Libreville, Gabon. I'd heard about that stop from Flemming who'd stopped close by there last year on his way from Europe to our

Earthrounders meeting in South Africa. Sao Tome is an island off the coast, a nice place, sea level airport but no avgas available. The distances were perfect and Gabon is right next door and has avgas. Actually, we could probably make it from Salalah to Gabon, without a stop in Djibouti. Hey, that's very doable, even without the consistent tailwinds across central Africa at this latitude. This is finally the right route.

June 10, 2008

Many of the components arrived today; I was busy with other things, but couldn't wait to start re-assembling the Mooney. So at about 5pm, I found time to open the boxes and get to work. Starter first. Since I'd changed three, count 'em, THREE, starters on my first trip, I knew how to reinstall the starter. Plus, everything on the engine is open without baffling, so it's easy to get at everything. Only four nuts, so on it goes. Well, it took a little more than that, but went on easily. I'll just have Art check the torque of the nuts. OK, now that the starter is on, I can time the magnetos. I'd put them on a few days ago and done rough timing, but with the starter in place, it's easier to do the fine tuning. I attach the magneto timing device, set the prop to the correct place and check the timing. It's a bit off, so I modify the angle of the mags, check again, move again, check again. There, that's pretty close. Enough for one evening, I want Art to check me as I go.

June 11, 2008

Art spends all morning with me checking, adjusting, and explaining. After he leaves, I head to Orlando for a podcast and a presentation to Women In Aviation. But, tomorrow I'll get to install the alternator and put all the baffling back in place. Also, we're ready to put the instruments back in the panel. It's starting to look like a flying machine again.

June 12, 2008

Phew, after an 80-minute phone conference with ALS and the fundraising team we all have our assignments and we're off and running. Immediately afterwards, I get a call from Universal

Arthur Miller, A&P, IA, confidant and friend.
Responsible for perfect airframe and engine operation.

Weather, the company that was offering to help with weather, handling in some countries, and other services. Judd was terrific as he'd presented my "adventure and need" to his upper management and was calling me with the final decision. They wouldn't be able to do permits or flight plans, but could help out with weather, long range forecasts for the trip and handling in difficult areas where I might need help. I was very thankful. I hadn't planned on help like this and it would be so much easier with their support. I was extremely grateful.

But, wow, what a day. Donations were over $106,000, fundraising was in full swing, flight planning was almost finalized and getting into the real details and we still had 24 weeks to go before departure. Everything was coming together.

June 25, 2008

I've flown the Mooney twice and everything is working well. It's a joy to be flying it again after the three-week annual inspection. I've been flying other planes, practically every day, but there's nothing like flying my Mooney. I've scheduled three Angel Flights over the next three weeks and a trip to Virginia to get some good flying in before heading up north to Oshkosh and onwards to Colorado and Idaho. July and August are going to be good flying months to shake any bugs out of the new equipment.

YES, we are going to do the 24-hour simulation. I'd received a call from a friend at EAA headquarters saying that they would not let us do it on their grounds. They don't let anyone, including their chapters, solicit donations during AirVenture. We were not to be an exception. We'd contacted Mooney as a backup plan; but, although they would give us the use of some booth space to promote our flight, we could not do a simulation. OK, on to plan 'C', the MAPA booth, Mooney Aircraft Pilots Association. They always had a plane in front of their booth, but Mooney had backed out of giving them one this year. So, Trey, MAPA president, liked the idea of putting my plane in front of the MAPA booth and would allow us to do the 24-hour simulation during the week.

During our last fundraising meeting; the idea of a sweepstakes, instead of a raffle, was suggested and accepted. It's difficult to do a raffle due to state and federal regulations. We could give away several of the donated items in a sweepstakes and gather LOTS of names and addresses for an email blitz prior to departure.

June 28, 2008

Today I get to spend ALL day on trip planning; well almost. I have to plan my upcoming Angel Flights as well, but that's still flight planning and FUN.

I'll start with the weather. I'd been watching it and downloading information last December, but wanted to get the average historical weather information for our stops and overflights, print them out, and review them with Carol at Oshkosh. Also, with the changing route over Africa, I hadn't looked at detailed weather in that area and we'd be getting closer to the equatorial, convective region.

With Universal Weather helping us out with handlers in various places, they need more information next week and I've just started communicating with Bo, my permit guy in Denmark, and he needs our trip information. So, I wanted to get everything up to date and detailed to send out to them and Carol. We'll have 24 hours sitting in the Mooney together at Oshkosh as we are planning a "24-hour simulation" while there. We should get a lot of discussion time.

What a day.... Immersed in weather, airways between stops, and much more detailed route planning. It's been great, very focused and tiring, but fun.

I have an Angel Flight tomorrow to the Bahamas; good practice with international flight plans and customs. All the preparation work is done, should be an enjoyable trip.

June 29, 2008

Well, it all started out well, but as I approached the first landing, my fuel boost pump quit. I hit the button to see if it would start again, but nothing. After landing, with everything quiet, I checked it again but it was dead. Hmmm, that's what these trips are for, to get the early failures out of the way on all the new equipment. After the first 100 hours, most equipment keeps going until its normal life expectancy. The majority of failures are either very early or late in the life cycle.

Still, not a good start to the day. I called my mechanic, Art, to get his advice. I knew the engine would start hot, as it was now. But I wasn't sure if I could start the engine cold without the boost pump. He said probably, but not to take the chance of getting stuck in the Bahamas. So I took the passenger to Ft. Lauderdale Executive, where others were gathering for this trip, and dropped him there to catch a commercial flight.

Once home, I took the boost pump out. I tested the electrical system to make sure power was getting to the pump, then I tested just the pump, nothing. OK, more UPS bills to get the part fixed. At least it should be under warranty.

June 30, 2008

Back to detailed planning. With all the routes, airways, and speeds, I could refine my date and time chart. We need to get into most foreign airports during their normal business hours. Let's see how it works out.

Amazing. I did two scenarios one with lots of rest time early in the trip, but night flying over Africa so as to avoid the worst turbulence and convective activity. The second was a stop, gas up and go scenario. I sent them off to Carol when completed. They both looked very good and doable. The difference was about 24 hours. One started a day earlier, but we took a good rest in San Diego, Hawaii, Guam and Thailand, then gas and go to fly at night over Africa, then a day flight over western Africa. When we get to Cape Verde, we could rest or go, depending on our fatigue and the winds.

The other only had a six-hour rest in San Diego and the remaining stops are gas and go. There may be some issues over arrival times being out of normal operating hours, but that occurs in Thailand where we are being met by friends and Cape Verde where we could rest before gassing up. We might be able to work around this issue and keep on schedule.

I'd contacted all the companies that had provided equipment, overhauls or other work for the Mooney during the annual inspection. I explained about the trip and cause and most of them reduced their price and I made the equivalent donation to ALS in their name. One company's owner's wife had been diagnosed with ALS. What a coincidence. He agreed that not enough was being done and there was little hope. His wife was seeing a doctor in New Mexico and undergoing a special treatment.

In June while giving a presentation on my first trip around the world, as often happens, someone has a friend with ALS. In this case, the friend had just been diagnosed with ALS and was researching it. I obtained the contact information for the doctor in New Mexico and forwarded it on. Because the ALS community is so small, it's contacts like this that lead to help and hope.

CHAPTER 4
TRIP TO OSHKOSH AND WEST

July 19, 2008

 I flew to northern Virginia, to a private air park, Dogwood, VA42, to visit Sue and Bill who were to be part of my ground crew for the trip. Bill had just completed a 2900 nm world-record attempt for efficiency, but fallen short by 100nm. They are also building a plane, a Lanceair 4, to do an around-the-world flight. We've been friends since we met in 2003 in England during my first around-the-world flight and their across-the-Atlantic flight in their first homebuilt Lancair.

They greeted me by radio and from the moment the door opened we were non-stop chattering about our different flights. Each side wanted to hear more about the other's endeavors than talk about our own. Finally after four hours we were ready for a break. We'd covered just about everything and had each helped the other with ideas and things to think about.

On to Indiana and a few days with Nancy, another pilot I'd met after my 2003 flight and with whom I'd stayed in contact and visited every year on the way to Oshkosh. This year she'll become a UFO, United Flying Octogenarian. That's a pilot who flies as pilot in command of her/his aircraft on or after the 80th birthday. Nancy turns 80 in October.

Nancy had shared her support of Hospice and other good causes with me over the years. This year she told me we were going to spend an afternoon with Chip and Jan Gulden. Chip has had ALS for six years and is bedridden. The afternoon flew by as Chip and I shared pilot stories, our histories with ALS, and our backgrounds in manufacturing; my previous company bought his company, Cummins', engines. Chip's eyes sparkle and his voice is strong; he

Above: Nancy and CarolAnn on her way to Oshkosh in 2007
Below: You can just see the sparkle in Chip's eye.

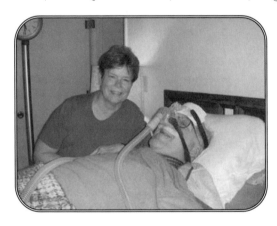

feels very lucky. What a strong person with a positive outlook. His outlook is very similar to Morrie in the book *Tuesdays with Morrie* by Mitch Albom and very dissimilar to that of my mother who was somewhat negative, in denial early on, and somewhat bitter at her predicament. Personally, I think it's wonderful to have Chip and Morrie's perspective, although I'm sure I would have a more negative outlook if I were to be diagnosed with ALS.

That day, while at Nancy's, I received an email from one insurance carrier that I was working with. It was a positive reply! Yeah. After being rejected by all the US companies and having lots of negative replies from a European company that was trying to get me insurance, I finally had a positive response. What a relief. I replied to Mary immediately and thanked her. I confirmed that yes, I would pay in full prior to departure (that was one of the company's stipulations). Mary joked that they wanted it paid in case I didn't return.

July 22, 2008

This morning I have an early departure from Columbus. After a quick hug with Nancy, I jump in. I have multiple stops today on the way to Oshkosh. First at Ft. Wayne with Gene and Lynne of Magnum Engines. Gene had overhauled my engine 700 hours ago in 2005. I was going to "drop in" just to have coffee and say "hi", but Gene said he'd give the engine a look over. Nick pushed the Mooney into the hangar and took off the cowling. They saw a little oil, dropped the exhaust, took off two intake manifolds and re-ground the surface to improve the mating. With new gaskets and hardware, they reassembled everything. In addition, Gene ordered a Challenge Aviation, KNN, air filter which he said would improve air flow and increase manifold pressure. I could install it when I returned home after this trip.

I departed for Saginaw, Michigan about 2pm. Overwhelmed is the feeling I have. What a morning; much more than I'd ever expected! Wow. Gene, of Magnum Engines, had given my engine a "once over" to backup Art's work and made some improvements. I was feeling positive.

It was a short one-hour flight to Saginaw. I'd filed an IFR flight plan as the weather didn't look that great. The automated weather indicated that all was fine but as I switched to Saginaw approach they said to plan for an ILS 5 approach as there was a rain storm crossing the field.

I taxied in rain towards the hangar and shut down in front just as the skies opened up. The linemen and Mark quickly pulled my plane into the hangar and I got out nice and dry when they were all soaked. Thanks guys!!

Mark had two 60-gallon ferry tanks designed and approved for his Mooney that he was letting me borrow for my trip. I wanted to put them in before the EAA AirVenture show in Oshkosh so that

Carol and I could see them, discuss the space remaining and our requirements for food, water, charts, etc.

After a quick greeting, I started unloading the plane and Mark brought the tanks along side.... They were BIG. Bigger than I had anticipated... I finished unloading and Mark explained how the plumbing worked and how we would do the installation. In less than an hour, they were in. But as I looked back and forth between the space remaining and my pile of stuff, I wondered if it would all fit. Putting the softer, squishy items around the sides and on top, I finally got to the big boxes and life raft, and it all fit, much to my amazement.

I was ready to go. On to Oshkosh. The storm had passed through as we worked; it was clear behind and looked good on the Wisconsin side of Lake Michigan. I filed another flight plan and was off.

Subdued was the feeling this time and, maybe a little worried. Not about the flight, but about public reaction. Looking at the tanks in the rear of the Mooney, taking up most of the cabin area; it could

Above and facing page photos show the rear and front of the tanks, respectively. There's not much room remaining up front for the pilots and the rear space isn't usable due to weight and balance constraints

be misinterpreted by non-aviation types and media. I was leaning towards keeping it and the windows covered while at the air show.

But, the objective of putting it in early would be met. It would be great practice for Carol and me. It was a much tighter fit than I'd imagined and we'd have to figure out how to pack and place our necessary equipment. The major problem would be the life raft. We couldn't leave it behind the tanks, where there was the most space, because there would be no access to it in the event of a ditching. The good news is that I had to have it refolded, as recommended by Winslow. Hopefully, I could explain the dimensions of the useable space and they could help us out by folding it in a non-standard fashion.

This leg will take me over Lake Michigan; no problem, right? Actually, I'm very calm and the weather is clear. As I head out, I can see the other side. I think back on my first crossing, back in 2000, three weeks after I bought my Mooney. It was hazy; I think I climbed up to 10,500 feet, so I could glide further in case of engine failure. I kept looking back over my shoulder at the land behind me. I couldn't see the other, west, side and increased the zoom on the GPS to see it represented, I was very nervous on that trip. I am very calm now.

I'm back to thinking about the morning with Gene and Lynne at Magnum. The combination of circumstances that brought us together is amazing...a Mooney pilot from Dayton came to a presentation in North Vernon, Indiana in 2004 and then asked me to return to Dayton to make a presentation to his flying club and EAA chapter. At that meeting he introduced me to Gene and explained that his engine had been overhauled by Magnum. I visited the factory during my stay, got to know Gene and his operation and liked what I saw. As my engine was almost ready for an overhaul, I kept the contact information and sent it there after we took it off the Mooney. We'd stayed in touch over the three years and during this trip to Oshkosh, he'd offered to look at the engine in preparation for the world trip. Amazing coincidences.

I can see land, not far at all. It's beautiful heading west...and there's Oshkosh, on the other side of Lake Winnebago. The tower clears me for the pattern and then landing. Not again, there's a rain shower off to the north. I think it's going to miss, but as I'm taxiing it starts raining. I really didn't want to pitch my tent on wet ground. Oh well.

July 28 - Aug 3, 2008 — EAA AirVenture, Oshkosh, week

This is the Mecca of aviation. I love returning year after year.

On Monday, we, Carol and I, started out with a photo session, video interview, and newspaper interview at the MAPA (Mooney Aircraft Pilots Association) booth. Then at the Mooney booth another newspaper did a photo session and interview. Wow, what a way to start the show. There we were in Tuesday's EAA newspaper, page 36, with a great picture and fantastic article. Many people stopped me on my one-mile walk from the campground to the MAPA booth to talk about our upcoming trip and visiting their EAA chapters and talk with their members after the event. Lots of Mooney pilots stopped by during the day, made donations, bought *Upon Silver Wings,* my book about the 2003 world flight, and chatted about the flight. It was a busy day.

Today, Wednesday, we have a hectic day, then get into the Mooney for a 24-hour simulation at 4pm this afternoon. It's going to be hot and humid, not the cool air we'll have when flying at 8000

*Carol and CarolAnn, feeling pretty upbeat,
as they enter the cockpit for their 24-hour simulation*

feet. But important to see how to fit everything, where all the wires will go, and figure out if we can sleep or not.

First a radio interview at 9am, meeting with McCauley and Lycoming at 10am, presentation in the museum at 1pm then return to the plane at 4pm..... what a day, but then, every day at Oshkosh is like this. If it's not for my project, it's volunteering at Flight Line Operations or the North 40 Registration. I love to watch the planes, meet the pilots, and, if any time is left over, enjoy the show.

We're both exhausted as we get into the cockpit at 4:16pm. We both just want quiet time after talking with so many people. We didn't try to rearrange things, but both put our heads back and rested. Greg from Arctic Air started installing one of his units to keep us cool. Wow, did that feel good. As soon as he finished, we both relaxed.

After ten minutes or so, we "hit turbulence" as Bill and Debey rocked the wings. Back to resting after waving to them and laughing. Then, after several more minutes, the rocking started again. I saw a video camera and pointed the people around to the other side. It was a local TV station and they interviewed Carol through the door opening. That went well, then we really began resting.

After a while, we started reviewing the electrical equipment we'd be using, lengths of wiring, movement required and where to keep everything. We decided to drop the idea of an intercom on the satellite phone. One person would talk, if necessary, and advise the other of the details afterwards. Splitting the output might reduce the volume reception and we didn't need that when some connections are not always the best. We figured adding a Garmin 496 on the co-pilot yoke wouldn't take too much wiring and could be kept neat. We'd shorten both headset wires, with tie-wraps, so they wouldn't be stretching all over the cabin.

Next we looked at the space available around the tank and talked about what would go where. Carol had the idea of making bags for charts, food, the laptop, etc. and attaching them to the top of the tank with Velcro. Easily accessible, wouldn't slide, and a good use of space. Oil could fit along each side of the tanks. Other equipment that we'd only need to access during stops would be along side, low down, or in the baggage compartment. We didn't want to put much back there as Mark said it really made a difference to the center of gravity and takeoff.

Food. Carol is an avid biker and was leaning towards Powerbars and similar foods for the trip. She'd brought a bag of assorted varieties for us to try. I don't like the smell of peanut butter, so we decided to skip those. I chose a cookies and cream Power Crunch. Wow, it was tasty and light. I only ate half as it was a snack, not dinner. We decided that two Powerbars and two pieces of fruit would be sufficient for each of us per leg. That wouldn't take up too much room. Where we weren't sure of replenishment on the ground, we'd carry a two- or three-leg supply, but that wouldn't be a significant weight or volume issue.

I demonstrated the satellite phone to Carol and she emailed Bill, one of our ground crew who'd visited us in the booth today. I emailed Sue, his wife. She responded that he hadn't made it out before the air show and would be returning home late.

We pulled out the laptop and reviewed the options for timing of the trip. I'd worked out two scenarios. One had more rest early on, the second was a gas and go scenario. Both had the same timing through the difficult countries after Thailand. After discussion and some modification, we decided we'd tweak the early rest option. From Carol's racing experience she felt and I agreed that adrenalin would keep us going for the first few legs. But we didn't want to be tired for the difficult legs over India, Oman, and Africa. So the more rest we could get early on the better. We'd both review possibilities, get together in Texas at the end of my continued travels after Oshkosh, finalize our plan, then I could contact Bo with permit requests as soon as I got home.

We had multiple visitors during the evening. Debey and Laura came along and helped us with a few details. We had "stuff" to offload into the baggage and other stuff that we needed from the baggage. Also they gave us an extension cord so we could continue using the laptop. Bill stopped by to see if we needed anything. Dave checked up on us. Linda and Carol from North 40 Registration stopped by while I was peeing..... I heard someone outside, so returned to a sitting position and saw who it was. They weren't sure if they should rock the wings or not. I laughingly thanked them and told them that everyone else had rocked the wings to wake us up!!

Debey called around 10pm to see if we were alright. There was an amazing amount of traffic on Knapp Road, right in front of us, going to and from Theatre in the Woods. It finally became quiet around 11pm.

Carol's alarm went off just before 6am. I said "That's OK, mine will go off in seven minutes." We were both half awake anyway. Carol felt pretty good and felt that she'd slept reasonably well. I felt that I hadn't slept well at all; but sometimes I feel that way but do fine during the day because the sleep was better than I thought. We'll see how I do. Breakfast time. I had an apple and Honey Nut Cheerios, Carol had a Power Crunch. I had my two No-Doz tablets instead of coffee. We'd both tried the pee bottle early in the night and felt OK at this stage.

We practiced with the satellite phone again and I continued documenting the simulation experience. Carol said, "Well, this is my regular schedule, and I'm going to have to get out. It's number two." We discussed regular bodily functions, timing, intake impact and what we'd eaten. I had very little for breakfast and no lunch yesterday, so I was still OK. Carol got out and went to the port-a-potty. Upon returning, she said that the good news was that her legs and back felt great, no movement problems. I said that she'd have to watch intake at home and get this figured out. Also that someone has suggested a large trash bag for situations like this. She agreed on figuring out timing and a solution.

7:30am. Not long to go now. We're both feeling OK, good about the simulation and test. Feeling good about space utilization. Potty functions in the flight suits look like the major issue. Looks like a relief tube going out near the front of the pilot's seat with a cap on it, stored between the two seats will work. If we each have a "Freshette" type anatomically correct adapter attached to a tube exiting through a hole in the left thigh of the suit and attaching to the relief tube, we'll be in good shape. We'll each work on that and test it in our respective planes. I'll install the relief tube in mine. Carol will test it with a bottle.

7:45am and the first MAPA booth worker asks how the night went. He starts opening up the booth and the pace of activity is picking up on Knapp Street.

9:16am we emerge, stretch, and start talking with interested observers. The two hours pass quickly, with no sitting down, and we're back in at 11am. We both want to rest first. The heat and non-stop talking is tiring. Again we praise Arctic Air for their air cooler technology for aircraft. We're cooler and more comfortable in here than everyone is outside. It feels great.

I have a list of discussion items. They are: crew resource management, instrument approach briefing, and how to say you are uncomfortable with a situation. Carol flies in a crew situation much of the time; I usually fly solo. Carol explained each of the items from her experience and we discussed how we would interact.

The five hours "fly" by and we emerge again at 4pm to an applauding crowd. We feel great. Jorge Cornish, an Earthrounder from Mexico, gets it all on video tape and we answer a million questions. It was a very necessary test, accomplished much more than either of us had originally imagined, and improved our chances of success. Debey brings us ice cream for our exiting prize. The next three days pass very quickly talking with more interested people at

*Carol and CarolAnn eating ice cream after the 24-hour simulation.
Talking with Jorge from Mexico and Greg from Arctic Air
(who kept us cool the whole time)*

the MAPA booth and meeting with more potential donor/sponsors. Carol heads home on Saturday and CarolAnn departs for Madison, WI on Monday. What an event, AirVenture, Oshkosh, WI. It's a real pleasure to participate as a volunteer every year and it's the best place to come for an exchange of information with other pilots and suppliers.

Several days later I'm flying to North Dakota to meet Norm, my Thailand contact. He is a Canadian living in Thailand who was going to meet me in Oshkosh. But that turned out to be the only week he could spend with his brother, which I completely understood. I hadn't packed my passport, so I couldn't join him after Oshkosh in Canada. Then, he called me and said that he could cross the border and meet me in North Dakota. I jumped at the chance. There was so much I wanted to review, face to face. Also, I hadn't seen him since his around-the-world flight, and I wanted to hear his stories.

Unfortunately, there were headwinds on the nose at 30 knots. I tried to stay low, but ATC kept moving me back up to 6000 ft. The

Norm Livingstone and CarolAnn at Pembina Airport, North Dakota

difference was 10 to 15 knots lower groundspeed compared with 4000 feet. I finally made it to Pembina airport. Not much to look at from the air. There wasn't much on the ground either, but the people were very friendly.

Norm and I sat on the sofa, I plugged in my laptop, and we reviewed my route and especially the details of the Asian over-flights and countries. Norm has lived and flown in Thailand for over ten years and he answered all my questions as well as offering his ideas and suggestions. Then we spent time catching up on his trip and chatting about our families. I was SO happy that we had time to meet and talk. It would make a great difference to the trip planning and execution.

I spent the weekend in Bemidji, MN as I had three days before my planned meeting and presentation to EAA Chapter 1446 in Big Fork, Minnesota. I caught up on emails and paperwork from our Oshkosh meetings and the fist-full of business cards with notes on them.

Then I settled down to work on the timing again. That was one of my biggest worries. Now with more information about our sleeping possibilities after the simulation at Oshkosh plus more specifics from Norm, I wanted to figure out several scenarios. I decided to fix the timing of the critical countries with entry and exit time constraints, then see how Guam and Thailand would fit with rest stops. I also did an expected speed and wind scenario, then a slow, light tailwind scenario. It worked out great. With everything moving along as expected, we'd have a seven-hour rest stop in Guam and a nine-hour rest stop in Thailand. If the forecast winds didn't look good, we could depart a little earlier and reduce the rest time. Thus the critical legs over India and Africa would remain in the same time window. I felt pretty good. I'll review this with Carol when we meet in a week. She was going to take a solid look at the wind charts to see if she agrees with my assumptions. We'll put the two together and finalize the schedule. Then I can get the permit process going with Bo as soon as I return home.

Overall, I'm feeling good about the trip. Every once in a while, I get some doubts. It's the thought of making last minute changes to the engine. That worries me. It's been working fine for three years since the overhaul. Now isn't the time to start changing things. At the same time, I had some proposals at Oshkosh that I'd love to see, especially the extra endurance and climb power promised by the proposed exhaust. I'm not sure how I'm going to work through this dilemma.

Aug 14, 2008 — Staying with friends in CO

I'm staying with friends in Ft. Collins, Colorado and giving a presentation to an EAA chapter during one of the evenings here. The local chapter loved the talk about first trip and were fascinated to hear about the upcoming adventure. They scheduled me to return in August 2009 for the next installment.

I'm still not satisfied with our stop in Africa. We can't go too far north due to headwinds. But, if we choose to stop in Gabon, we're heading into the rainy season and convective activity. Although not impossible, it could add complications to the trip. I start looking for other options. Focusing in on Chad, I find the capital, N'djamous as a possibility. One site says it has avgas, another says only jet fuel. Chad has areas that are acceptable for tourists and is in the dry, Saharan section. I send an email to Paula at Universal Weather to see what they can tell me about this airport as a potential stop. The flight timing would be better, with a shorter leg from Oman and a slightly longer leg to Cape Verde.

I'm also thinking that we'll ask Bo for multiple overflight and landing permits and see which is best based on winds as we're traveling, then make the call. I like to have options. I'll talk with Carol then see what Bo can do when I return home.

Aug 20, 2008 — Visiting Universal Weather

I flew to Spicewood, Texas, yesterday, where Carol lives. We had planned to visit Universal Weather today. Our project had been assigned to Foxtrot Team and they and we wanted to meet face to face, and to discuss more details of the project. What a day! We talked about the route, refueling, countries, plane, and many other topics. Where we had "holes" or yet unknown data they had answers. Their systems are terrific. A quick phone call and they knew where avgas was available and who could provide it. We were awed, amazed, and most grateful that they had offered to work on our project. When we departed, we felt even more confident that this adventure would be a success.

The day was also planned for Carol and me to practice some instrument flying together. There was bad weather all around, so it was perfect. I flew to Houston, Hobby, with an ILS approach, and landed just before a storm hit. The very nice people at Enterprise Jet Center didn't have any tie downs, but put my Mooney in their hangar until the storm passed. Carol flew the bumpy return leg with an approach into Austin prior to returning home to Spicewood. Overall, it was an extremely successful day. Now we need to finalize some of our decisions.

Aug 21 - 22, 2008

We spent two days together as tropical storm Fay was pummeling Florida and I couldn't get home. It was time well spent. We reviewed our optimum route and chose Chad as our "final decision" for the stop in Africa. We are still going to keep our options open, get permits for other countries and check into Carol's contacts in Cameroon. Depending on weather during the trip, that will allow us to make the decision en route to Oman.

CarolAnn and Carol with Judd, Suzanne, Jerri and Paula from Universal Weather, Foxtrot Team

I crunched all the numbers on my flights and gas consumption since leaving Florida. Although I'd run pretty consistently at 10.4 gph on the JPI engine monitor, the actual consumption was 9.3 at 6000 to 8000 foot altitudes and 9.1 over the mountains. So, we really had more margin than we thought. With the exception that we don't yet know how much the fuel consumption will increase during the hours we are over gross.

We'd already spent quite a while discussing the long leg from Hawaii to Guam. That's the leg with the least options. The winds are consistently good, strong tailwinds, with one exception, last December 5th there was a low pressure just to the west of Hawaii giving what would be 34-knot headwinds. When Carol factored that into our calculations, we'd have an average three-knot tailwind for that leg, instead of a conservative average of 11 to 15 knots. Dilemma — would we depart if those were the actual winds?

If we ran the power settings more conservatively, we could average 8.5 gph and have an endurance of 25.9 hours. With the worst winds we saw, our flight time would then be 21.6 hours; so, we'd have a safety margin of 4.3 hours. Our other option is to use the Marshall Islands as an alternative stop. Unfortunately, they are closed on weekends and would charge horrendous overtime fees.

Also, they only have 95 octane car gas and 130 octane aviation fuel. It is a last option, but one we really don't want to exercise.

So, after all the discussion, we feel pretty good about making Guam. We will start off with a high power setting to get to cruise altitude. After using fuel and dropping weight, we'll back off on the power to conserve fuel. When our consumption rate shows a safety margin of three hours, we'll start enriching the mixture to increase speed. We'll be watching the time to destination and fuel remaining figures closely during the entire leg and will only breathe easy once it's "in the bag."

I felt much better after having discussed each leg with Carol. It was no longer just my decision and my routing; she bought in, added ideas, and was 100% part of the final decision. I felt better.

August 23, 2008

I had planned, and filed my flight plan, to fly across the Gulf from Houston to Florida. The range was not a problem and, although I didn't have the HF installed, I did have the satellite phone with me. As I approached the coast, Air Traffic Control started to ask my destination and route. One guy obviously knew where Ocala was and said, "Good luck crossing the Gulf." I had to smile at that; he didn't know what else we had planned!

The next few controllers started changing the routing. They wanted to keep me closer to shore. I accepted their routing and stayed over the Gulf, but headed east to the New Orleans area. At that point the airway took a southeasterly heading toward Sarasota. At several points I was out of communication and radar range. But, ahead of time, ATC had given me another frequency and location to contact the next controller. Each time it worked. Four hours later, I was over land again and deviating around thunderstorms on a typical Florida summer afternoon. Within half an hour of reaching the coast I was home. What a five-week trip. No problems with the plane or engine and lots of good statistics on fuel consumption and air speed and different settings. Overall, a successful series of flights.

Unfortunately, the arrival home was not as successful. There was no electricity, no water, no Internet or cable and the car and motorcycle wouldn't start..... welcome home! I later learned that there had been a severe lightning strike, very close, several weeks previously. Everyone had lost power and cable. It didn't take long to get the electricity working again and put the plane away. The horrible job was cleaning out the stinky fridge and freezer!

Universal Weather's Jerri, seated, Judd and Paula
demonstating some equipment to CarolAnn and Carol

Above: Earthrounders' meeting December 2005 in Mexico. Flemming from Switzerland, with Bill and Sue Harrelson from Virginia, and Claude from Australia. **Middle:** Flemming and Angela, foreground, in Switzerland with Lec and Norm visiting their chalet during Norm and Lec's 2007 around-the-world flight. **Bottom:** Wes and Sandy, left side, with Bill and Sue at their home in Florida.

CHAPTER 5
FINAL DETAILS AND ROUTING

Aug 29, 2008

 With 14 weeks to go, we're into the final details. I had to get the route and dates finalized and send them off to our permit guy, Bo, in Denmark. I thought the routing was pretty close, based on what I'd done previously; but after a long ten hours I finalized the route, with two options to Thailand and Oman. It had been a day of frustration and elation. Although I had picked rough airway routing previously, this time I had to check everything to make sure it worked. I'd think I was there, then find that the leg over Laos had a Minimum Enroute Altitude (MEA) of 25,000 feet. This is not possible in the Mooney. We might be able to file the route, but once we arrived, if their Air Traffic Control (ATC) people asked us to climb to 25,000 and we couldn't do it, we'd be in trouble. I found one route across Laos with an MEA of 8000 feet. The only problem was that it was not in line with our route. We'd have to deviate over 150 miles to cross at that point. I found a more northerly route from Guam, to get to that point. Unfortunately over the Philippines we'd have to cross between two airways. That's not always acceptable to other counties either. Things that we know we can do in US airspace are not always acceptable elsewhere. I'd have to find a route that worked, then ask for deviations, if possible, along the way. After many hours, I had good routes across Asia and India, but not Africa. There are no low level routes. We'd have to ask for forgiveness or fly VFR, visual flight rules, instead of IFR, instrument flight rules.

Tom stopped by. He had offered to help and we'd worked out a device that he could build. Kind of a backup to other systems, belts and suspenders, but in this case, very important. It is an independent barometric alert device. We'll set it when at altitude. If the barometric pressure changes, i.e. we lose altitude, it'll set off an alert in our headsets. So, in the unlikely event that we both fall asleep and the autopilot fails, and we lose several hundred feet in altitude, it'll wake us up. We'll test it on the way to Arizona along with all our other tests.

September 2, 2008

Frustrating. I'm trying to avoid future problems by checking out the flight plans ahead of time. Do you think I can get through to someone on the phone? New York Oceanic is the group we'll be talking with while crossing the Atlantic. I'd like to make sure that what I file is what they really want me to fly. Especially after crossing the Gulf a week ago. I filed the flight plan, received the clearance, as filed, then Houston Center started changing the routing. We don't need this while crossing the Atlantic and Pacific. So, I've been trying all morning to talk with someone about crossing the Atlantic. I've been passed off over six times and the last guy hung up.

Wow, I finally spoke with a live, knowledgeable guy. John Foster, now retired, but formerly the Boston Center operations manager who had "welcomed me home" on my 2003 trip. We'd stayed in touch and visited several times in New Hampshire and Florida. He'd just emailed me a number to contact New York Oceanic. It worked, Pete, was superb. He knew what he wanted and what I needed. I added a few latitudes and longitudes to my flight plan and all is well. Or at least it should be.

Last night I think I did half the trip in my head. I wasn't dreaming, but I was "flying" across various countries speaking with different controllers to make sure the flight path was OK. It would seem that my planning has also invaded my sleep time.

Now that's two nice controllers in a row. I just spoke with Dennis from Oakland Oceanic. He was helpful and figured out, after a couple of questions, that we were going around the world. I explained that since this was a world-record attempt, we didn't want any problems with clearances and wanted to checkout all the flight plans prior to departure. He wished us "good luck with the flight."

He also pointed out that Wake Island could be used in emergency. I'd just seen that in the Pacific chart supplement that I'd been reading. I rechecked the route and there was a waypoint, AWK, right over Wake Island. Good to know, just in case; at least a safe landing point even if they don't have fuel.

We'll be testing the route across the Gulf in October, so those are two legs confirmed and the third will be flown. I've emailed a 99 in India to start checking out that leg. I've also emailed a pilot, contacted through Lane Wallace of *Flying Magazine* fame, in Chad for confirmation of our Africa flight plan. The more we can checkout and confirm ahead of time, the smoother the clearances should be. Let's hope anyway.

Michael also got back to me by email. He could sign off my tanking with 10% over gross, assuming all the paperwork was correct. This would allow us to do some cruise calculations over gross weight and find out by how much our fuel consumption would increase and by how much our airspeed would decrease. We'd still have to extrapolate to 15% over gross weight. But, it would give us more data for computation.

September 3, 2008

Well, well, well, some things work out after all. The 99,woman pilot, contact in India forwarded the email to another 99 pilot who asked for the details and will look into it with Air Traffic Control over there. It sounds like they may well funnel low level traffic further north. Good to know ahead of time, so that we don't start heading south and then get deviated further north, wasting time and fuel.

Then, I ran into an English friend here where I live. He had a contact in Africa and was going to look into Gabon for us. I advised him that Gabon was no longer a stop and we are looking into Chad. He has an English friend who does low level flying and surveying work there. He'll give me his contact information and see if he can help. Some days things go right and other days, things go wrong.... I'm smiling today.

Yesterday I was starting to ask myself if I'm getting into too much detail. Do I really need to get every flight plan approved ahead of time. Do I really need to get into all these details? OK, so

I'm a bit over-controlling, I like to know what's going to happen ahead of time and don't like to get caught off guard. I'll keep getting into the details as much as I can.

Off to Daytona Beach to give a presentation about the 2003 trip to a Women in Aviation chapter there.

September 4, 2008

I took off the magnetos this morning. Unison, the manufacturer, had issued a service bulletin after finding some early failures. My serial numbers were on their list. I called and talked to a knowledgeable technician. He said they were mostly early failures and if I had over 50 hours, which I did, there probably wouldn't be a problem. I explained the upcoming trip and we agreed that opening them up and looking at the carbon brushes, then making a decision, was the best course of action.

I took the magnetos (mags) off and over to Art's where we opened them up. We'd never seen so much carbon dust. There was definitely undercutting and they would have to be replaced. I called Joe, the Unison tech, who ordered two new mags.

Art and I were shaking our heads. This was outside the game plan. We were to get 100 hours on all components to be over the "infant mortality" stage and into the high reliability portion of the life cycle curve on all components. With two new mags, I'd get another 50 hours on them and we'd take another look. That wasn't part of the game plan either; we just didn't want to be "fiddling" with components just before departure. But, right now we don't have a choice. Earlier, Art and I had decided to forgo the exhaust system that had been offered. It was just too late to make changes. This one, with the mags, had been forced upon us.

September 7, 2008

Wes, my HF guru, and Sandy, his wife, a pilot and ham operator, dropped in for 24 hours of hard work. He'd prepared the HF kit and we wanted to install as much as possible for early testing.

Well, that was a useful, very full, and beneficial 24 hours. We tailored the antenna mount for the belly panel. It looks good and will cause less drag than my old one. Wes installed outputs for HF power, HF communication through the headsets using the intercom, and an input connection for another component that another friend, Tom, is designing. The extra electrical gadgets are coming together. We also decided to rig a support under the seats to hold the HF radio, tuner and digital box (for emails). This would keep them close to the power supply and up front for weight and balance, but out of the way.

September 11, 2008

I've been working on routing all week. With a great contact, Saudamini, in India talking with the ATC, we now have a solid flight plan across India. The new question is whether to stop in Nagpur or not. After going back and forth in a few emails, the timing doesn't work out except to stop at night in Nagpur. Saudamini advises me that there is some fog in December and January in early morning. Back to plan A... but, we'll continue with permits to allow for that as a backup plan.

But at least the planning is getting more solid. We're looking good all the way to Djibouti. Our only remaining unknown is crossing Africa. Ten weeks to go.

September 19, 2008

Finally up and running, guess I should say flying, again. Feels great. Flies great. Love this plane. Now I need to get 50 hours on the new magnetos before December. Good job I have some short trips around Florida to do. Off to an Angel Flight meeting tomorrow, down to Punta Gorda to get my Winslow life raft refolded and look into a smaller one, then off to Lakeland for tanking later next week. I'll find more trips to get the hours on all the accessories.

I started looking into obtaining charts for the trip. I contacted my previous chart source. Dave had shipped charts all over the world in 2003 to make sure I had current charts everywhere I was flying. Unfortunately, he sold the business and the new Dave doesn't stock the same charts. Also, the Department of Defense, DOD, which used to print instrument charts for the whole world, discontinued their service. On top of that, the number one chart supplier, Jeppesen, has charts for everywhere, but only sells full countries or continents, i.e. Africa. I need about 5% of any continent's charts, so I really don't want to buy and waste all those charts. They also decline to give or sell me just the charts I need for the trip...bummer.

I'm going to contact friends in Europe and other pilots who work for cargo carriers. I'll find a solution.... Somehow. This isn't going to stop us.

September 23, 2008

What a relief, I just got my new third-class medical today. I went to get it early because the worry has been eating away at me. My eyes seemed to be going downhill and I really didn't want glasses/corrective lenses listed on my medical just yet. It wasn't due until November, but I just couldn't wait any longer. Anyway, I made an appointment and flew over today. My left eye was slightly worse, but my right eye was better than two years ago. That's why I thought things were going downhill, it was an exaggerated difference between the two... I feel a whole lot better and enormously relieved. One more box checked and out of the way before our trip.

September 25, 2008

We have a life-raft problem. With the tanks in the back and two people up front, there is no room for my four-person Winslow life raft. There is room behind the tanks, but it's too far to the rear for weight and balance requirements and it's not readily accessible in case of ditching. It's recommended to have it up front, ready to go out the door in the unlikely event of a ditching.

So, I'm down in Lake Suzy, Florida, with Winslow LifeRaft Company. I brought my current life raft down for servicing, but also wanted Charles Daneko, my contact person, to look at the space available and see what options are possible.

After a tour of the factory, which always appeals to me as I spent 30 years in manufacturing, we looked at the rescue raft option. This is a four person without a canopy and only one inflatable ring instead of two. But it folds to a much smaller volume and could fit behind the seat. We met with Gerard Pickhardt, President of Winslow. Charles explained about my trip, and I saw worry on Gerard's face. I assumed that he was thinking of liability and was about to back out. He said I was the pilot, they were the survival experts, and started recommending an improved rescue raft, two rings, a laser signaling device and stabilizers under the raft. Charles explained about the limited space, but Gerard insisted on doing what he could do to maximize our survival options. It was amazing to watch the thought process.

After explaining about ALS, my mother, the first trip, and now this trip, Gerard started talking about his association with ALS. The person he knew didn't last very long and went downhill very quickly. He asked about research and a cure. I explained that no pharmaceutical companies are working on a cure. It's an orphan disease. Not enough people have the disease to make it profitable for research. So ALS Therapy Development Institute, with its 31 scientists and $6 million a year budget, are the leading researchers into the cause and cure for ALS. Gerard said they would do what they could to support my flight. I thanked him and we shook hands.

So, the kind people at Winslow serviced my raft and Charles and I took the refolded demo survival raft to see if it would fit. What a company: US materials, US workers, US made. It's good to see manufacturing staying in the US. It is a pleasure to do business with them. I also learned that 90% of the business jets have Winslow life rafts and they make and service the slides for some of the airlines. One was inflated in the shop. I asked if I could slide down it, but Charles laughed and said no.

We placed the rescue raft behind the seat and it fit with room to spare. Charles and I took pictures and measurements. They'd be able to look into the two-ring raft with more safety features and still fit it into this very small available space.

Off to Ft. Lauderdale Executive Airport for an Angel Flight meeting, then up to Cocoa Beach to stay with Wes and Sandy for the weekend and make more progress on the HF installation. The magnetos are working well and the plane is flying great. The only issue is the "clanging" of the tie-down straps against the tanks. It's a little unnerving. I keep thinking something on the plane is making a noise. Think I'll wrap the straps when I get home and see if that reduces the noise.

September 27, 2008

Unbelievable ... I'm working with Wes, installing HF equipment in the plane; I'm doing the simple job of installing the supports for the radio under the seat. Wes is fitting the power supply under the instrument panel. When a call came in. It was a $5,000 donation to ALS. A former business associate, who had helped me with permits across India in my 2003 trip, called. I'd sent him a package a week ago to advise him of my trip, so that he heard it directly from me and not second hand. His mother-in-law had just died from ALS and he wanted to make a donation in her loving memory. I thanked him profusely and indicated that we could put whatever dedication he wanted on the web site. I was blown away; wow, this was exactly what we needed. I couldn't get over the call, I was elated. Finally, I got back to the job at hand, but couldn't stop smiling.

But, why was it that people touched by the disease are the only ones making big donations? It's easy to see why they do, because they know the impact on the patient and the entire family. I didn't do anything before my mother was diagnosed with ALS. It's very difficult to imagine the impact of this disease, to see a vital, usually young person with a bright future diagnosed, then become entombed in his/her body. The brain works perfectly, it's just that he/she can't move. Finally, the progression moves to the lungs and the person dies of respiratory failure.

Nothing could stop my happiness and appreciation of Nelson Cambata's donation and it made me want to redouble efforts to get the word out to others. Too many people have been affected and there is no cure. So, back to work now to get the HF in and get the plane ready, then do the flight, then set out on the speaking circuit to get the word out and bring in more donations. Thank you Nelson, we need more people like you.

Catherine stopped by later; she's president of EAA Chapter 724. She jogged my memory about something I'd forgotten. Many people ask about the accents and how difficult it is to understand controllers in foreign countries. I had thought at one time of taping our transmissions. But, with everything else going on, I'd forgotten.

She explained how it could help to have video of action on the ground and audio of transmissions. She's right, it's not just aviation, it's the whole story of our trip around the world that interests people.

Dedication to Nelson Cambata's mother-in-law on Mooney fuselage.

CarolAnn giving a presentation to EAA Chapter 74 in Orlando, FL

CHAPTER 6
TWO MONTHS TO GO

October 1, 2008

 This was the news I was dreading. I received an email from Michael, the DAR* who was going to have the tanks installed and sign off the 10% over gross for our flight test. His email said that his FAA adviser had a problem with the documentation. I called Michael and said his email "sounded bad." He said it was and could he call me back. He was in the middle of a conversation.

I'm waiting on pins and needles with a sick feeling in the pit of my stomach. I can't believe this is happening again. Two weeks before my first trip in 2003, Globe Aero, who was doing my tanking, called to say the FAA was having a problem with my trip. This time I'd already sent the documentation to the FAA in Orlando, over three months ago, and followed up with several phone calls. Each time, my contact, Al, said that things looked good and he should have final confirmation shortly. Now this...

Well, in my mind, I've worked out a routing with 10% over gross. It'll require a few more stops, but it's not impossible. I have to quit thinking like this; there has to be a solution. I just can't stand the wait.

Later, Michael called me back. He asked me to copy and mail all the documentation. As the FAA would be signing me off for 20% over gross, after his 10% over gross sign-off, his adviser wants to make sure everything is perfect. Well, that doesn't sound too bad. Actually, very logical. So, I sent all the paperwork to Michael and waited.

---

* DAR. Designated Airworthiness Representative. Arm of the FAA doing inspection under FAA authorization.

October 3, 2008

Well, some great news from Norm in Thailand today:

> Sent: October 3, 2008
>
> Subject: Progress in Thailand
>
> CarolAnn - The note below is from the President of SGA to the President of NOK Air. We are getting a good response from SGA who have contacted NOK Air (subsidiary of Thai International) for their support as well. NOK would be good for the clearances, flight planning, customs and all that kind of ground work.
> Although I have not talked to Dr. Jain of SGA directly they seem to be well on board and I'll expect to see him within the next week when I get back to Bkk.
>
> Please feel free to ask any questions or I can call you if you'd like to discuss anything
>
> Regards
>
> Norm
>
>
> Dear P'Viratnkul krub,
>
> There will be a charity flight with attempt to fly around the globe piloted by Carol Ann Garratt within 7 days. The aircraft is scheduled to stop in Bangkok on December 7th in the morning. Carol is raising U$1M. Her tentative schedule is in the mail below. She will arrive 0600-1000Hr and plan to leave 1600hr on the same day.
>
> SGA decided to support for requested tools filter, oil, and spare parts at cost. Her aircraft can park in SGA's Don Muang hangar.
>
> It is a good opportunity for SGA and NOK to support this charity.
>
> Please advise if Nok's flight ops team can support to ICQ clearance at cost + flight clearance paper work filed for 1600Hr? It is important that she won't get delay due to the race.
>
> Please advise.

This was fantastic news. Our Thailand stop and maintenance was well under control.

Norm and NOK team in
Bangkok, Thailand

Norm sent me a picture of himself and the NOK team who would be working on our project.

With Art, we've finished putting on new tires and completed a retract test. He thinks my relief tube idea will work, so we'll fabricate that and install it this afternoon.

I ordered the avgas to be delivered to Oman today. The contact, Vinod, emailed back and said he'd already heard about the flight. He'd get the latest prices to me by early November and that shipment would be no problem.

Nine weeks and counting down. Things are really coming together.

October 5, 2008

Wes was working like a beaver all weekend finishing the HF installation. He'd also designed and wired a "cockpit voice recorder" using a small Sony recorder. That way we'll be able to record all intercom, ATC, and HF communication during the trip and put it on a CD. Lots of pilots asked what international communication was like, now they'll know. Hopefully Carol and I won't make too many verbal "bloopers" during the seven day trip...

Then we went up for the flight test. We were headed to Bill and Sue's air park home just northwest of Suwannee County airport in Florida. Along the way Wes talked with his brother Bill and the communication was very good. We did a "low pass" over the strip so that Bill and Sue could give us feedback on how the trailing wire antenna and drogue were hanging down and moving. Well, they couldn't see it. Wes wasn't worried, it was small. So Wes started

Wes in his usual position in the cockpit, upside-down.
He's working on HF wires under the seat

reeling in the antenna while I did another turn around the pattern and got ready to land. Well, well, well, there's a reason they couldn't see the drogue, as Wes reeled the wire ALL the way in, the drogue was gone.

Over lunch, Bill said the wire was flapping up and down with an amplitude of about ten feet. Wow, that's what happens to wire when there isn't a weight on the end. Bill and Wes fashioned a temporary drogue with an orange funnel so that we could do more tests on our return flight. During the low pass after our departure, Bill and Sue said it was hanging down about 25 degrees, ten feet below the fuselage, and staying pretty straight, no flopping around.

We continued on and tried to reach our HF parties in Virginia, South Carolina, and Hawaii. Unfortunately, the frequencies were extremely busy and we couldn't hear anyone we called. Wes talked with the Marine Net controller from 50 miles north of Toronto, excellent transmission and reception. Then I pulled out the charts and asked Wes to tune in Houston Oceanic frequency, 11,396. I'd be crossing the Gulf in a few weeks and it would be nice to have this checked out ahead of time. I make the call. Immediately New York Radio replied and said they would relay to Houston. I explained that I was a Mooney over Florida and testing my HF unit as I would be crossing the Gulf in a few weeks. The controller said that our transmission was "five by five." Her transmission was loud and clear to us. I thanked her and "high fived" with Wes. I was pumped!! The frequency was clear and the communication was perfect. An excellent test.

Wes was able to get one more test communication completed with Charlie, who lives across the street from me. This was perfect also. Excellent work, Wes, 100% positive. The only minor problem was that the Sony recorder was active the whole time due to alternator noise. It's supposed to be voice activated, so we'll have to work on the sensitivity to reduce the total recording time.

October 8, 2008

I was updating the diary when Al called from the FAA. I was all ears!! I held my breath and listened to what he had to say. Finally I released my breath. He thought it was going to be OK. He'd looked at the paperwork, talked with the FAA person in the Great Lakes region who had signed off Mark's over gross flights (owner of the tanks), and said that it looked like we could get a 10% over gross for the test flight and 20% for the record attempt. I was relieved, a little. Still worried until I had the piece of paper.

I rode my bicycle over to Art's to give him the installation paperwork and talk about the sign-off. He said that if Al said it was OK, I didn't have to worry. I talked about a leak check, although Mark had already done a pressure test. Art said to fill the tanks and let them sit. I started that process the same afternoon and felt better right away. I loaded one tank with 60 gallons and let it sit until the following afternoon. Then I siphoned the fuel into the second tank and let it sit another day.

I also used the time to practice siphoning with a new 5/8" ID hose that I'd just obtained. In Salalah, they have no pumps and we'll have to gravity feed the fuel from the 55-gallon drum sitting in the rear of a pickup truck to the plane's fuel tanks. Therefore the practice session and checking the timing, i.e. how long to siphon a gallon multiplied by 55 gallons per drum. Looks like two gallons per minute. Not bad, less than an hour for both drums. Then neighbor/pilot Joe drives up to chat and catch up on the trip. I told him my lips were tingling from siphoning.... He told me I didn't even have to suck to get the fuel started. Just put the complete hose in the 55-gallon drum, fold over the top few inches to stop air getting in and it leaking back into the tank, and lower the hose into the plane tanks, then release....now where did he learn that? Anyway, I tried it later and it worked! I feel much better about the whole Oman stop and fuel transfer process.

Working on the decision points had been on my mind for a few weeks now. I finally sat down and started working it out. It turned out that the easiest calculation is how far we fly on the ferry tanks in the rear. We climb on the left wing tank, then cruise using the rear tank first. When that's empty, we know exactly how much fuel is remaining. By calculating our distance to that point, along with our TAS (true air speed), the wind speed, and fuel consumption, we know how much further we have for endurance. The main assumption here is that the winds remain the same. This is a good assumption across Africa and the Pacific. It's less sure across India and on the final leg across the Atlantic. Off the east coast of Florida winds are often westerly, giving us a headwind for the final few hundred miles.

Carol called three times this week. She is upbeat, confident, and pumped. Her contacts in Guam got back to her and will help us out. The Cape Verde contacts will support our fuel stop and waive the airport fees, great! She'll be here in a few weeks and we'll do the test flight.

October 9, 2008

More "stuff" comes together today. Satellite phone tests, HF tests, and backup transponder. That's been on my mind and on a list somewhere for a long while now. I finally got it done, well almost. My neighbor, Fred, always told me about how he kept a spare transponder under his rear seat. I was thinking THAT could stop us where ever we are, if the transponder goes out, we go no further. If I could borrow one for the trip, an extra pound of weight could really save us. Fred's is identical to mine. I'll get it tested and certified in my plane, then we'll be good to go. Thanks, Fred.

October 11, 2008

More pieces of the puzzle falling in place today. I flew to Spruce Creek, across on the east coast of Florida, near Daytona Beach, to give a presentation to the 99s chapter. They asked tons of questions and were highly interested. Then Marcia asked about O2 levels and altitudes. I explained that we'd have oxygen, but could only get it refilled in Thailand, therefore had to be careful in using it. At the same time, we had to measure our O2 levels and be on oxygen at altitude and at night. I said that I'd contacted a nurse who was going to try to obtain an oximeter for us. Marcia said that she had one and that we could borrow it. She went home and delivered it to me before I departed!!

October 19, 2008

It's getting down to the final decision making time on weight and balance and how much gas we're taking. Due to two light females up front, we can't fill the tanks in the rear. Even if we put all our heavy items at the co-pilot's feet, we'll be aft CG if we fill the tanks. I had already determined that filling the tanks isn't easy. We'll have to leave an air space on top so as not to flood the cockpit while filling. That's already a few gallons down from the maximum capacity. But now that's a moot point.

The only option is to add a 20-pound weight tied down in front of the co-pilot's seat. I really don't want to carry "dead" weight, but it will allow us to carry additional fuel. To stay in balance that's going to be the solution and still we'll be limited to 110 gallons in the rear tanks rather than their capacity of 120 gallons and 20 gallons in the outer tanks instead of 34.

Due to carrying less fuel than I had originally planned, I've detailed each decision point on the long legs. This task took all yesterday afternoon and this morning. At each point, I'm typing the winds, fuel consumption, time to the check-point and fuel remaining. Based on current ground speed and fuel remaining, I make a decision, HARD AND FAST. No second guessing this decision in the air. Each time, my heart pounds, my breath gets short... I can feel the "get there-itis" and I'm sitting on the ground. I KNOW I don't want to stop in Mumbai, India. But, if the fuel is below a certain level and we're behind schedule due to headwinds, we MUST stop. I know we'll want to get back to Orlando International in one leg across the Atlantic Ocean. But, if there is low pressure over Florida and westerly winds just to the east, it'll mean a gas stop in the Bahamas. I write down every calculation, way point, fuel remaining, and ground speed for the point where we recognize that we might be running late. Again at a second point confirming that things aren't going well and at a final decision point where we will turn the plane, head to Marsh Harbor, and inform others of our decision and new ETA. Each of these decisions is difficult on the ground. Carol will review them on the ground, then we will not deviate.

October 20, 2008

It's the day for everything to start coming together. Saudamini's charts from India arrived today. I needed those early to get them in a shipment to Norm in Thailand. We can't carry everything. So, I'm shipping stuff to him for the second half of the trip.

Also received the update for the flight planning software. This is the last one that will give us the most current data base for the whole world in the computer flight planning software. And, Kabir's DVD of our test flight with Panasonic recorder arrived. Wow, what great pictures. I can see why he loves using that recorder while flying. It's a great way to share the adventure with non-flyers. We'll get lots of raw footage and make a DVD of all the countries as well as incorporating parts into a future presentation to pilots and civic groups.

Tomorrow is the BIG day. I get a knot in my stomach when I think about it. The FAA is coming to inspect the tanking and plumbing. Their sign-off is imperative for this trip to work. It's what I've been impatient for and dreading at the same time. I hope I'll be able to sleep tonight. Well, it'll be over, one way or another, tomorrow.

October 21, 2008

The FAA visited today to inspect the tank and plumbing installation. Art came by with the paperwork and to answer questions. I think I held my breath the whole time. I was able to answer a few questions and Al, from the FAA, said he had talked with the FAA inspector who had signed off Mark's installation.

They reviewed the weight and balance calculations, looked at where everything would be stowed and said this would be a two step process. First it was OK to proceed with our test flight at 10% over gross; we would complete the paperwork for that flight. Then, we'd review the results and proceed with the second sign-off for the December flight.

After they departed I let out a sigh of relief. I didn't feel the euphoria that I'd expected. I thought I'd be jumping up and down for joy. Huge relief, nothing more. Maybe because we're getting down to all the last details and there's so much to do. Hopefully the euphoria will come later, definitely after the flight.

October 22, 2008

Along with other jobs, I decided it was time to cut the relief tube to the correct length and test it a few times. So, I donned my red flight suit and kneeled in my pilot's seat. I checked that the tube would reach both seats and inserted the Freshette into my suit. I connected the two tubes inside my pant leg and started peeing. I put a bucket of water underneath and I could hear it dropping in. When all was complete, I detached everything and started the cleaning process. Then I noticed my pant leg was wet. Hmmm. I'd tested the connection on the bench and it never leaked. I must not have completed the seal between the two tubes when it was inside the pants. Time to do the laundry and try again tomorrow.

October 23, 2008

I contacted the graphic artist who'd done the cover, layout and pagination for my first book. This one was going to be on a tight schedule as I had speaking engagements starting next February. I didn't think we could complete it by then; but wanted to shoot for March delivery of the books.

We exchanged a few emails and she felt it was doable. She was also excited about the trip and gave me a price reduction as all donations for books were going to a charitable cause. I thanked her profusely.

Later in the day it was time for the relief tube test. I determined that I could poke the end of the Freshette tube outside the leg of the flight suit so that I could verify the connection. I tested it twice and it worked fine both times. Problem solved. Check off that box. We'd be giving it the real test next week on the way to Arizona and back. My worry was hitting something in the cockpit with flailing arms and legs as we try to turn around in the seat. At the same time I believe that this little exercise would be good for circulation. We'd just have to be careful, especially at night.

I had the bladder of the Camelbak sitting flat on top of the tank. The tube hung down and was simple to reach for a sip of water whenever I needed one. This way we wouldn't have bottles rolling around in the cockpit.

October 27, 2008

Busy day, fly to Punta Gorda to pick up the Winslow life raft. They had designed and built a raft JUST for our trip. They wanted to keep us safe. Wow. I met Charles on the ramp and he proudly showed me the new raft. It fit perfectly behind the seats. Thank you so much, Winslow management and employees.

Next to Merritt Island for Wes to complete the HF installation. We got all the little items finished and tested the new little laptop and HF in the air. 100% successful. Back home.

Great results today. Five weeks to go and things are coming together extremely well.

I'd received the FAA special flight permit earlier and started reading the details. Hmmm, slight modifications will be required to our timing. There are two pages of necessary limitations required for flying over gross. I fully understood the need for them. The main one was day only flying during the time the plane is over gross. Very logical. Well, I'd review the implications with Carol after her arrival tomorrow.

October 28, 2008

Watching www.flightaware.com, I followed Carol's progress across the Gulf. She arrived on time and parked in my neighbor's ramp area. We unloaded her plane and moved her stuff into my spare room.

We had a lot to catch-up on and I'd made a check list of the major items we needed to review. So, we covered all the subjects and had a full evening. As we were going to be flying through the next night, I suggested that we sleep as late as possible the next morning and not set an alarm.

October 29, 2008

The next morning was full: sitting in the cockpit, reviewing the fuel system and valves, deciding where to store equipment in the cabin, reviewing the weight and balance, and getting ready for the test flight to Arizona. We had very little fuel in the rear tanks, first we'd have to make sure the fuel lines didn't have any air in them, then while flying, Carol would run the rear tanks dry and quickly switch tanks. I'd done it a few times and wanted her to get used to the procedure. After that we'd fill the tanks at a local airport with low priced avgas and fly to Orlando International to meet the FBO where we would depart and return.

Finally we were ready. I pulled the plane out and closed the hangar door. As I was getting into the right seat, I pointed out the Spot tracker to Carol and showed her how to turn it on. The lights didn't come on, so I went to the baggage compartment to get new batteries. I remembered packing them somewhere. Not finding them in the rear, I returned to the cockpit and started looking around. I finally gave up. I'd already tested the Spot tracker and didn't need to test it on this flight.

I buckled up and closed the door. Carol read through the check-list and started the engine. We taxied to the end of the runway and did the engine runup. Carol advanced the throttle and started rolling down the runway, took off and started a slow left turn. I felt a breeze on my neck...

I looked back and saw blue through the baggage door. The door had blown open, it hadn't been shut and latched correctly. I told Carol the door was open and to fly around the pattern and land. She did everything perfectly. We saw some sun shields on the runway, so I asked her to taxi back and stop and I'd pick up the parts.

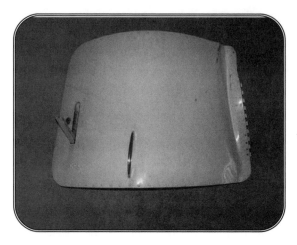

Bent baggage door

When I got out, I looked at the baggage door and felt sick to my stomach. The door was creased back and crooked. I knew immediately that it wasn't repairable. I was sick about the Mooney being damaged and upset that we'd have to cancel the flight and the presentations that had been planned.

We taxied home and put the Mooney in the back corner of the hangar, it wouldn't be flying for a while. Several people came over and gave advice. Carol called her Mooney maintenance contacts in Texas; my A&P, Art, came over to take and look and make a recommendation. Another pilot, Dick, brought a list of aircraft salvage yards that we might call for parts.

We sat down and wrote down some of the checklist items we'd been talking about writing down. We certainly didn't need a second problem later on. Then we talked about what might have caused the misstep. I'd climbed into the cockpit many times and not forgotten to close and latch the baggage door. What changed this time?

We made more calls. Many places knew right away they didn't have the part. Several went to take a look. Mooney called back to say they had the part in stock, part number, and price. Well, we had one option already. I finally reached a salvage yard that had two doors. Wow, he'd go out and re-check, then call me back. A thousand dollars later (vs. new for $2700) and it would be shipped tomorrow. I felt better.

Carol and I decided to make best use of the time by sitting in the cockpit and deciding where items should go. I had been uncomfortable in the right seat, knowing that we needed to fit in more stuff and I was already out of space.

I sat left seat this time and Carol right seat. We started with the equipment in the same uncomfortable position. Then we started moving stuff. There was plenty of space under the pilot's legs without encumbering any movement or getting in the way of the controls. We moved the 20-lb weight and the oxygen. That left much more room on the right hand side. That would work for 60% of the legs. Only the three very long legs needed the life raft up front for takeoff, to improve the weight and balance and move the center of gravity forward, due to extra fuel being added for the long legs.

The life raft fit where the oxygen had been. It was difficult to move. But we persisted and several times moved it behind the seats, as we would after fuel burned off. We also simulated removing it in the event of a ditching. Although difficult, we both felt much better. We'd need a test in the air, but this was doable.

Then we pored over a calendar and finally determined another time for flying together and testing takeoffs over gross. Based on our timing, we'd be able to do more tests and maybe get more accomplished. So, overall, we felt not too bad.

Well, I still feel badly about damaging my plane. But, some good came out of it and we accomplished things that we wouldn't have otherwise.

Carol and I had a wonderful Chinese dinner with a superb curry and great stories. We both learned more about the other and I certainly felt better later in the evening.

November 3, 2008

I've been really calm since the baggage door incident. I knew that I was getting "hyper" and wound up, but this problem has somehow managed to get me calmed down about the whole project.

Once all the logistics for the door replacement were in place, I started doing maintenance on another plane and spent little time working on the flight. Maybe that's what I needed, time off.

Anyway, this morning I practiced drilling rivets out of the old door, in case we need to remove the door hinge and replace it. Now I just have to wait for the new one to arrive.

I reworked the flight timing, due to the FAA limitations on the special flight permit. All over gross flying must be day only, so our schedule had to shift by about 12 hours. We'll depart earlier, at night, at gross. If we need a fuel stop, no problem while crossing the US. After that, our departures will be mid-morning and our arrivals will be about midnight in most countries. We'll actually get more sleep early in the flight, a nine-hour stop in Hawaii and Guam. We still have the maintenance stop in Thailand, but there will be more rest for me.

Yesterday I met with the Orlando marketing group over breakfast. Chris is going to start the marketing campaign to get local involvement early. Dave is planning on being our media communication person during the flight. With that kind of coverage, I have nothing to worry about.

Al from the FAA just called. His "higher ups" have limited our over gross to 115%. That's OK. I'd essentially expected that and actually felt better with that limitation. I'd done several spreadsheets with that maximum number and knew it would work. I explained our little problem from last week. He understood and would issue a permit for the new test flight. Great, we were still a go.

I was working in the hangar when the UPS truck stopped. I knew it was my door and started walking towards the truck. Yep, the box was the correct size. I carried it into the hangar, opened it up and aligned the hinges.... It lined up, it fit!! Well, it was too large all the way around, but that was a good thing. We could trim it to fit.

I biked over to Art's with the news. He came over to look at it and agreed. We'd start on it first thing in the morning in his hangar.

November 4, 2008

I taxied over to Art's hangar, we lined up all the tools and work space and got to work. I was amazed, in two hours we were over half way there. Fitting, cutting, fitting, grinding. It was starting to sit in place correctly. After lunch we completed the job. I was ecstatic. I wanted to go flying. I had other tests to do, try out Fred's backup transponder, review the new Jeppesen world wide data base, but really I just wanted to fly again. Off I went for an hour and felt great.

November 5, 2008

Ocala Style magazine has set an appointment to interview me this morning. I assumed that pictures would be taken, so spent the first few hours washing and waxing my Mooney. Gleaming in the sun, it looks great.

When Krissy arrived, we had a terrific interview, but she said pictures would come later. Oh well, I can wash and wax again.

I needed some night time flying so went up this evening. I flew over to Ocala airport and did some take offs and landings in the dark before returning to Leeward Air Ranch. I wasn't as comfortable as normal at night, so decided that to get more night flying in before our departure.

November 6, 2008

Flying "under the hood" with, Fred, my neighbor and right seat safety pilot, this morning. With all the maintenance and down time for tanking, I haven't flown enough instrument approaches. We'll get some in today, some next week and more before the trip. I want to be in peak condition, instrument flying and night time flying, everything must peak just before departure.

November 9, 2008

After two days of volunteer jobs for Angel Flight and Young Eagles, I'm free to head to Cocoa Beach to meet up with Wes and Sandy again for the final/final installation and changes to the HF system. We'll also review the computer interface and other electrical gadgets.

This afternoon everything went very smoothly with Wes and soon we were headed home for computer updates, software verification, and a terrific dinner and conversation with Sandy. It just seems that we've been all work and no play over the last few months. So, we agree to set a time, early next year, to get together just for fun and conversation, no work involved, besides flying or sailing.

November 10, 2008

Monday morning Wes drops me off at the airport for an early departure to Fort Lauderdale Executive Airport and Premier Aviation. It was a superbly clear, cool, morning with 50 miles visibility and no-one else in the air. I thoroughly enjoyed the one-hour flight south.

Another Wes, a former Mooney employee and very experienced Mooney pilot, has scheduled my 406 ELT, Emergency Locator Transmitter, installation in the Premier maintenance hangar. The new ELT is an improvement in locating a downed aircraft with more precise latitude and longitude information going to a satellite and being fed back to ground receivers. Also each ELT is designated to an aircraft, so it's known immediately who is down and where. But, for me the major reason for the installation is weight savings. The old ELT is five pounds at 121 inches aft of the datum. The new one saves three pounds which calculates to .1 inch in center of gravity movement forward. With the weight we are carrying, I need all the forward cg movement I can get.

Eddy is efficient at removing the dorsal fin and installing the antenna. Manny has the more delicate wiring job, but completes everything by noon. Wes gives the engine and airframe the "once over" with his experienced eyes. We have a short list of items to receive slight modifications prior to departure. I'll do that with Art over Thanksgiving when we're doing all the other final maintenance checks.

The return flight was peaceful. Feeling good as things are coming together. Feeling good that Wes had confirmed the plane is tight and in good shape. Feeling good that the systems are working and we're getting close to departure. Beautiful flight home.

November 11, 2008

Carol calls to say there's a front which moved in, across Austin, quicker than forecast. She doesn't know exactly what time she'll depart.

Several hours later I check flightaware.com and there she is, already underway and scheduled to arrive at 5pm.

Since we have to depart early tomorrow morning, I'll load the plane ahead of time and leave the luggage by the rear of the plane so she can see and weigh what's going in there. I have the weight and balance spreadsheets prepared to review. I want us both to understand the configuration and options we have. This evening we'll review everything.

November 12, 2008

We're both up by 7am anticipating an 8am taxi out. Carol reviewed the weight and balance analysis last evening and knows that her takeoff will be with the center of gravity right on the rear limit. I've put extra weight in the baggage compartment to make this happen. As we add more fuel, the cg will move back to that point, so we want to test it early and at lower weight levels. We'll "sneak up" on our final 115% weight little by little and feel and measure how the aircraft responds at each step of the way.

We're loaded and ready to go. I think I've checked the baggage door four times. We start and taxi out. The first test is to let the rear tank run out of gas and have Carol watch the fuel pressure, hit the fuel boost pump and change the fuel selector to the left tank. I've run the rear tank down, so that we won't have to fly for over half an hour before this happens. But still, it feels like an eternity. Carol circles a neighboring airpark, out to a lake to the south and back to a lake to the north. Out and back, out and back. The fuel pressure needle wavers a few times, then finally, it starts down below the green, this is it... the engine coughs, Carol hits the boost pump and reaches down and changes the fuel selector knob. The engine catches and runs smoothly. "Wow, that really stops the heart," says Carol. That's the first time she's done it. I say, "It stops my heart every time. I never get used to it."

Actually, Art has recommended that we don't let it go "all the way to coughing" but try to switch just as the pressure goes down. Then we won't have to clear the lines before the next flight. It makes sense and that's what we plan on doing. But it's a very small window of time and if neither of us happens to see it at the exact moment the pressure drops, the engine will cough. So, we have to practice it both ways.

Now we head to Orlando International Airport. We'll meet with Operations Manager Michelle Hartmann and Air & Space Television, a new TV station, just getting funding to start a new cable network.

Orlando tower gives us a tight turn onto the runway and has a plane a few miles behind. No worries, it's a long runway and our

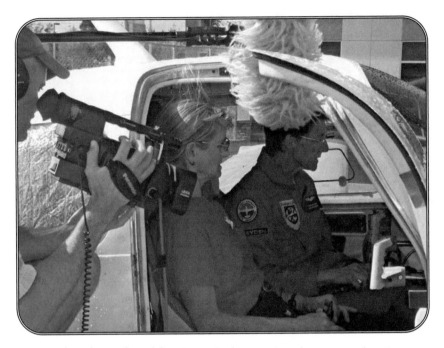

*Being interviewed in the cockpit at Orlando International,
prior to the test flight*

FBO is over halfway down. So, we touch down and turn off. There are David and Phil waiting to meet us. Dave flew with me during part of my 2003 flight and is helping with media communication locally in Orlando. Phil is CEO of the startup Air & Space Television who planned this interview today.

With handshakes and introductions all around we're ushered into a meeting room that has been setup with cameras, lights and boom mike...no time to think, we're being interviewed right away. I guess that's better than getting worried about it.... After half an hour of questions and answers, we head out to the plane for a walk around and explanation of the specifics of a Mooney and the changes necessary for our extra long legs over the oceans.

After an interesting interview with Air & Space Television and a chat with customs to explain our plan, we were ready to depart Orlando International Airport on our test flight. Carol was sitting left seat, so I called for our clearance. The person asked that I verify destination and to confirm that we wanted to go to Key West VOR first (that's two hours the wrong way prior to starting to head north). It's understandable that he was a little confused, so I confirmed our intention. We finally received the clearance and taxied to the end of the runway.

The wind had shifted to the northeast, so unfortunately we actually had a quartering tailwind for departure. Carol kept the plane on the ground and called out the airspeeds. After 70 knots it started getting light, and just flew off the ground very smoothly. I forgot to look at the exact takeoff distance, but it was less than 4000 feet. Our climb rate was very good at first, over 500 fpm up to 4000 feet.

Somewhere after departure, another controller asked for confirmation of our routing, thinking that it had been input incorrectly. We laughed each time; they were actually trying to help and couldn't understand our indirect routing.

It was magnificent looking down over the Gulf and Key West. We turned around Key West and headed north. As we headed up the east coast of Florida, the controllers started asking for more waypoint information. One asked if we were the same Mooney that departed Orlando International several hours ago and headed to Key West and didn't stop en route. We replied affirmatively. We could see him scratching his head...

Finally a controller said that our transponder wasn't working. This was my neighbor's transponder as mine had just died and was in the shop for repair. Well, transponders looked like they were going to be a problem. Better to get the problems out of the way before the trip. They let us continue and we just called out waypoints as we flew.

I entered position reports into the HF system as well as sending test emails and emails from the satellite phone. All systems were working well and GO for launch.

After we reached our cruising altitude of 11,000 feet, we switched to the rear tank. We had put 55 gallons in there and would measure how long it would take to run dry. That would give a good calculation of our fuel consumption while over gross. Based on estimates, we would almost be at our destination when the tank ran out.

The clouds cleared as we headed north, but we knew there was another system to the northwest headed our way. There was an undercast over South and North Carolina, but it cleared as we reached Raleigh-Durham. Into Virginia and the tank finally ran out of gas. Carol hit the boost pump and we switched to the right tank.

We were given instructions to descend and finally landed at Stafford, KRMN, at 8pm, after seven hours and 40 minutes of flying.

Bill and Sue called on the radio and we followed them to the hangar they had obtained for us. The scales were already there and they'd set everything up for the official weighing with Art, from the National Aeronautics Association, in the morning.

We unloaded the plane, loaded the car and headed to their house for dinner. Sue announced the menu, which sounded delicious, and we realized how hungry we were. Two things we hadn't done well, hydrate and exercise. Exercise each hour was listed on the hourly checklist, but we'd really only accomplished it about two times each. We'd have to be more diligent at that, and add 'drinking water' to the hourly check list.

Dinner was fantastic as always. The wine was excellent. And, the conversation lasted until midnight. There was so much to cover.

In the morning we watched the weather. It wasn't supposed to move in until late morning. Maybe we'd get the weighing done and have time to exit the area before the worst of the storm hit.

We got the scales set, loaded the plane with gas and Art arrived right on time. Unfortunately, the rain arrived at the same time. The hangar was a blessing. We closed the door and still managed to roll the plane on to the scales. We weighed it twice for confirmation. Art took pictures to confirm that all the equipment was in the plane, then Carol and I were weighed. OK, so we'd each put on a pound or two, most of that was the life vest we were wearing...

We all chatted with Art about records, the NAA, and flying. Bill was working on a different record and was building a plane for yet another record, so they had a lot to discuss.

As the weather was bad, we couldn't fly over gross, so we offloaded the fuel and checked the radar. It looked like it'd pass through in another hour, so we headed off to lunch.

The ceiling was at 400 overcast with some drizzle, but the storms had passed through and we headed southeast to clear weather. There was only the chance of one other thunderstorm, which was to our west as we passed Savannah. I was flying and Carol was practicing with all the electronic equipment. She posted position reports, sent and received emails and started working with the satellite phone. But, ATC decided they needed information at

Official weighing of plane and pilots, note the ramp and scales behind the wheel. The reverse 'L' is the HF antenna exit point and drogue.

the same time and it was already night time, so we stopped training and worked on ATC data.

We did much better on exercising on this leg. Each time we read the hourly checklist, we started our exercise routine. Drinking water was still lacking, but this was a short flight. We'd do much better on the real flight.

We landed at 8:20, tired but content. The tests had gone very well. After putting everything away, we debriefed over dinner of fruit and cheese. I was exhausted and went to bed. Carol was wired and stayed up a while. It's good that we're reacting differently, we want to be on different schedules as the flight unfolds.

Carol checks the weather and it looks like headwinds for the trip home. She's certainly had a lot of Mooney seat time, six hours on Tuesday, over nine on Wednesday, almost six yesterday and another seven today. She's really feeling good about how things are coming together.

As the day goes by, I track her progress on Flight Aware, unfortunately, with the headwinds, she has to make a fuel stop. Next year she plans on adding the Monroy tanks for longer range flights.... She's hooked.

With all the data we collected from the test flights, I spend all weekend crunching numbers. Although tighter than we'd like, everything is still doable. But, we've gone from an exceedingly comfortable margin to a slim safety margin. All that's calculated without winds. When adding in a positive tailwind, the margin is slightly better.

The most worrisome leg is from Hawaii to Guam. We only have one optional stopping point and need to make that decision over Wake Island, with 1900 nautical miles completed and 1303 left to go. We'll have some more good fuel consumption data after the legs to San Diego and Lihue, Hawaii. Those will give us increased confidence; but, as we stand right now, it's still a GO.

Chapter 7
Ups and Downs of the Last Two Weeks

November 17, 2008

 Guess I'll be going through some ups and downs over the last two weeks. I just received an email from Bo, the permit guy....

Sent: Monday, November 17, 2008 7:45 am

Subject: YEMEN !

Hello CarolAnn,

Rather bad news on the Yemen permit. As per the agent working on it, I'm now told that application for this should be made directly to the Yemen Embassy in USA. CAA Yemen cannot issue the permit. I'll be writing them in a minute, and let you know any progress on this.

Bo

I checked the planning charts immediately. It would be possible to depart Oman to the northeast (the wrong way), return to the India airspace boundary, turn south, then cross into the Mogadishu, Somalia airspace then to Djibouti. That would stop our chances of continuing the same day across Africa, but would keep us going if the permit doesn't come through.

I departed for St. Augustine just after the email arrived. I had a Rotary Club meeting and presentation. My "twin Mooney" pilot had invited me to speak. It was a terrific group, very interested with lots of questions, who made a collective donation of $260 to ALS.

Upon returning home, there was another email from Bo:

Sent: Monday, November 17, 2008 1:07pm

Subject: Re: YEMEN !

On track and in contact with the Embassy. A bit
confusion, but it looks like I can get things done
through them. Rest going well according to plan 1.

Need your decision on Niger, if I can skip that permit.

Bo

I felt a little better. This would resolve itself.

I'd promised ALS-TDI that I'd have another newsletter draft by today, so I set about writing the latest updates.

November 18, 2008

Pretty busy day today. After a noon telephone interview with AvWeb, I'll fly to Leesburg to meet Phil and Brad for an air to air photo shoot and we'll land at Orlando Executive. There Chris has set up a media afternoon for interviews with the local TV stations. That evening I'll be giving my Orlando EAA chapter an update on the planning for this trip.

The whole day went off without a hitch. Except for being VERY bumpy down low, we did most of the air to air filming at 5500 feet in nice smooth air. The approach and landing at Orlando Executive went relatively well for me. However, when Phil and Brad landed they informed me that they were bumped around like crazy (they were flying low, parallel to me to film the landing) and probably didn't get a good shot of the landing. Oh well. Everything else went well.

The night flight back home was smooth and quiet. I relaxed and was glad the busy day was over.

November 21, 2008

After two days of flying with friends and teaching Civil Air Patrol cadets, I got back to the planning details.

I've been flying the Mooney and Lycoming engine with Gami injectors and testing "lean of peak" settings. For the first time, with the new Gami injectors, the engine runs smoothly with low power settings and 7.0 to 7.6 gallons per hour mixture settings. As I put these new numbers into the long leg calculations, it looks like we can make the distances without winds. But, we're pretty confident of having at least 10-knot tailwinds and with luck, 15- to 20-knot tailwinds.

After a few email exchanges with Norm and Bo, we have a slight modification over Thailand and Myanmar and Bo has most of the permits. There are only a few permits outstanding and Bo feels they will be issued in time. I'm never happy with last minute issues, but can't do anything on this front except wait and hope.

My neighbor, Fred, and I did more instrument approaches and night landings this evening. All went well except the last VOR approach which was a little off. We'll look at the charts on the ground and review tomorrow.

November 22, 2008

I'm trying to load the FliteStar discs on to the new small computer I bought for the trip. Jeppesen's product, FliteStar, is a great route planning program and I wanted it with me on the trip. But, the old laptop is just too bulky for the small cockpit with two pilots and all our equipment. So, I bought a mini-laptop for the trip. Being mini, it doesn't have any drives, so loading software is more difficult.

Other work behind the scene

Numerous other things have been coming together or falling apart over the weeks. I'd been collecting international enroute charts and was using contacts everywhere, Saudamini in India, cargo pilot friends, and Earthrounders. It wasn't complete, but was coming together pretty well when I received an email from Jeppesen. I'd contacted Eric at Sun 'N Fun, but they couldn't donate to charity, only locally in Denver, CO. So, although we talked about product and service donations, it didn't seem to go anywhere.

After two emails, we recognized the error in communication and Eric offered to provide charts and software updates for the world. Wow... that was a huge help. We put the Jeppesen logo on our website and I would donate the equivalent (to what I'd have paid for charts) to ALS. One more problem solved.

Art, my mechanic, had a carbon monoxide (CO) detector that he was going to start using on all planes after annual inspections. He wanted me to test my Mooney on the long test flight. Well, unfortunately, it went off. Only during climb, not in cruise, but on the floor it measured 18ppm and up to 48ppm as we climbed. At mouth level it was also reading 48ppm.

This was serious. As another friend, Doc, a former doctor, did the calculations, he explained the CO effects are cumulative and more dangerous at altitude. The only remedy is pure oxygen, not dosed as we take it when flying. So, we had to find the cause and fix it.

Two other local Mooney pilots took the CO device and came back with zero reading. It had to be something with my plane and maybe the HF installation.

First I tried covering the antenna hole, but the next flight the reading was 26ppm.

November 23, 2008

Off to Naples, Florida, to meet with Kabir who's lending me his super duper, high definition Panasonic video recorder for the trip. Over the months, he has insisted on teaching me how to use it, buying extra cards so I won't worry about recording all takeoffs and landings and interviews in the plane and on the ground. He believes it will enhance the presentations and be a good selling and PR tool.

Looks like he's 100% right as the TV and cable channels are now asking for video and pictures en route. Hopefully, we'll be able to download in Thailand and get the video from the first half of the flight back to US for immediate use.

We chatted over lunch and I went through exactly how to use the recorder, change and charge the battery, change the discs and copy the discs on to my laptop. We had already done a test flight and Kabir had placed Velcro on the glare shield in the correct spots for the best shots.

On the return trip home I tested the HF antenna and radio again. Wes said to keep testing it at all opportunities. I reeled it out, chatted with a few folks, then started reeling it back in. It felt a little "funny" reeling it in, maybe stiff, but certainly not smooth. Finally it was in, but the green mark wasn't there and the wire was all in strands. I assumed there was a knot stuck underneath. Well, hopefully it wouldn't be dragging on the ground.

Upon arriving, I looked underneath and indeed there was a huge knot. The drogue had come off and the wire had entangled itself again. Quick email to Wes... not good. Just over one week before the launch and this was a major set back.

Later in the evening I called Wake Island Operations. Wake Island is a US base on a small atoll in the central Pacific Ocean. I spoke with a very nice and helpful young man, Chris. He advised me that we can't list Wake as an alternate. I explained that it wasn't our alternate; Majuro in the Marshall Islands was listed on the flight plan. But, that I wanted to know if, in an emergency, we could land there. He said yes, in an emergency. I felt better already. There was someone there 24-hours a day and they would turn the lights on for us!! Sounds like a commercial. I said that it was a very remote possibility; but that we would be flying overhead and would it be OK to call in? He said that he was on swing shift that evening and would be happy to hear from us. I gave him our names and tail number. I wouldn't mind landing there just to say hi!!

November 24, 2008

Little pieces came together today. I taped up some ports to retest the CO on my next flight tomorrow. The Pacific Chart Supplement was received. It's got tons of good information on airports across the Pacific Ocean (like Wake Island).

Wes sent a map of the world with the Winlink stations; so we'd know who to connect to while flying to download our emails and pickup any that had been sent to us. I got the 406 ELT registered. And, the ALS webpage was ready to receive daily updates.

November 25, 2008

Got my "flight" haircut this morning. Boy is it short!! Well, there are several days and nights that a shower is out of the question, so short is the best way to keep it. Don't even need to carry a comb... saving on weight.

Then I flew across the state to pick up a new tracking device. This is new to the market and the designers wanted to test it on my flight. Happy to oblige if it'll give good tracking information to those following the flight on the web page. It looks pretty interesting and won't require any intervention for the whole trip. I'll charge it, stow it under the seat and forget it until the return.

Upon my return, I started the final maintenance checks. An oil and filter change, air filter cleaning, spark plug cleaning, gapping and rotation, mag check and general overall inspection. Art came over to look it over before I cleaned it up.

November 26, 2008

What a discussion!! With Judd from Universal Weather, we'd set up a phone conference with their "weather guru," Dave, for 2pm this afternoon. Not quite into the forecast period, he wanted to see what major questions I had and review what he was seeing and planning on giving to me during the trip. Wow, what depth of knowledge and detail of what was happening around the world at the latitudes I'd be flying. He'd been watching some tropical storms in the western Pacific and over India; I'd seen them also. It was late in the season for this, but he said nothing major was forming, the Inter Tropic Convergence Zone (ITCZ) was to the south of our route and not likely to cause any problems.

He looked at the winds at 5000 feet and 10,000 feet between Hawaii and Guam. He recommended that after about one third of the distance, we consider climbing to 10,000 feet as we'll get stronger tailwinds from that point to Guam. Great stuff.

He knew our course over India, one of my worries as I'd seen the winds change a great deal as we headed northwest over Nagpur. He said the normal winter cycle would most likely give us easterly winds over that part of India, which would be perfect.

We briefly touched on Africa and the Atlantic. He said that three days before our return he could give us a good reading on the Atlantic and if we'd have headwinds or tailwinds as we approach Florida. I said that we have plenty of options for fuel stops if it turned out to be headwinds. But, it sure would be nice to know ahead of time.

I felt terrific and in good hands as we hung up. He'd reinforced much of what I thought over the Pacific and added more details than I had. He'd also covered a lot that I didn't know about Asia. I was looking forward to working with Dave throughout the journey. He seemed to be fascinated by the project as well.

Doc came over to review the latest information on CO tests. Not great, but not bad either. He'd also learned that we can get our Carboxyhemoglobin (COhb) count from the monitor. He wanted me to test that next flight to see what it would be after a climb. The other option was to have blood drawn en route to check the COhb count. Not an option that I wanted to take.

Then Wes and Sandy arrived. They were going to stop overnight on their way to a family Thanksgiving and Wes had new wire for the antenna. Although they arrived later than planned, Wes wanted to get that installed and ground tested right away. Although a stiffer wire, it looked like it was going to work.

I'd started taking baby aspirin this morning and reminded Carol, by email, to do the same thing. This was numerous doctors' recommendations to start thinning the blood a little to avoid clotting during the long flight legs.

Thanksgiving, November 27, 2008

Wes finished his tasks this morning and they departed with BIG hugs. I might not see them again until my return.

I finished the engine work and did a test run. Everything looked good.

I exchanged a few emails with Norm. He was in Canada and his reservations had been canceled and he wouldn't be able to make it back to Thailand for two weeks. Certainly not in time for my trip. In addition to that, Bangkok airport had been closed for two days with no news of kicking the protesters out and opening the airport. Also, Mumbai, India was on lockdown due to terrorist activities. The India permit was still pending and I had to overfly India. It could be that that permit wouldn't be issued..... Not very good news.

I also sent an email to Bo with some options on routing if permits didn't come though. We certainly were looking at a whole set of problems with less than five days to departure.

November 28, 2008

Exhausted this evening after lots of, hopefully, final tests today. The HF worked great and the new wire on the reel wound smoothly both out and in. I'd tested it at altitude and was in the airport flight pattern turning downwind to base when I remembered that I still had the trailing wire out. So, I climbed out, exited the pattern, and wound it back in.

The satellite phone didn't work. I'd done plenty of tests and today it squealed with each call. Couldn't talk, let alone hear myself. New problem to fix.

Flew with Art, my mechanic, he said it was the smoothest four cylinder he'd ever heard; and that's saying something. We were below eight gallons per hour and it ran smoothly, lean of peak. He checked everything out and pronounced me ready to go.

The CO readings were much lower, even with three climbs to 6000 feet. The total Carboxyhemoglobin percentage was 0.1%. When Doc received the news, he pronounced me safe and ready to go.

Later, I called on the satellite phone outside of the plane. Worked fine. Then I called on the satellite phone in the plane with it running, on the ground. Worked fine. Then I plugged it into the plane's intercom system. Still worked fine. No squealing. OK will have to try again while flying.

Earlier in the day, I'd receive emails from Norm and other people, including the presidents from Nok and SGA, in Thailand. They all recommended going to Chiang Mai. I changed the flight plans and emailed the necessary people to highlight this change. Bo had already started changing the Thai flight permit. He indicated that the Cambodian permit was due this weekend. That only leaves the India and Yemen permits as potential show stoppers. Unfortunately, with the terrorist activities, it wasn't sure that the India permit would be issued.

Still, everything else was on schedule for a Tuesday departure.

November 29, 2008

No new news today on Mumbai or Bangkok. Norm hasn't got a ticket home and Carol won't come to Florida until tomorrow evening due to weather.

I get the tool bag and tools sorted out with Art. He lends me some of his and gives me a list of everything I should carry.

Another Art lends me his transponder, so I'll get that checked and signed off for the Mooney on Monday.

November 30, 2008

Final flight planning today. Cross checking the Jeppesen enroute charts with the FliteStar data base I've been using for flight planning. There are more details on the enroute charts, so I modify the flight plans slightly. I'm also arranging all paperwork by flight legs to keep the cockpit organized.

The weather in New York is sleet and drizzle, so Carol pushes back her flight another day. That's going to be tight to get her up to speed. Oh well, nothing we can do about the weather.

December 1, 2008

It's the last full day before departure and tons of people are sending emails, phone calls and dropping by the house to wish me well. Carol is in flight and will arrive this evening. I just started to get a cold yesterday, sore throat, etc. It's getting worse today.

I'm explaining to many people that not all the permits are in yet, but we feel they will arrive and we're planning to depart as scheduled, Tuesday afternoon from home, Tuesday evening from Orlando International. We've given the media a two-hour window to do interviews at Galaxy FBO prior to our departure. I've also taken the last hour as "quiet time" to get our heads on straight after interviews and to get ready for the flight.

I'm at the door talking with a neighbor when Bo calls. If we can fly at 16,000 feet, Yemen will issue the permit. I say, "Yes, we can fly at 16,000 feet." He'll get that permit today. OK, another one done. Only India left to go and Bo feels it will come in.

"Twenty years from now you will be more disappointed by the things that you didn't do than by the ones you did do.... So throw off the bowlines. Sail away from the safe harbor. Catch the trade winds in your sails. Explore. Dream. Discover."
–Mark Twain

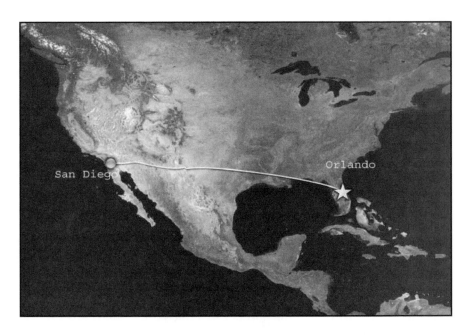

Actual flight path by TracPlus Global Ltd.
Actual flight time, 16 hours 41 minutes

Chapter Eight
Here We Go

—Leg One—

Tuesday, December 2nd, 2008
We're off... (030132z[1], 8:32pm local time)

 Well, it's been a long day. It's 11pm and we're just south of Pensacola, FL. Carol has just turned the controls over to me and is covering herself with the blanket to try to get some sleep. Carol arrived late yesterday evening. This morning she reviewed all the charts and flight plans for the whole trip. She only had a few questions and understood where we were going and what we were doing.

I was finishing the final details, loading the plane, strapping down the borrowed transponder that had just been inspected and signed off for our plane. I emailed all the lists, phone numbers and contacts to everyone and took lots of calls from the media. We were to take off from Orlando International, at 8:30pm, but had given the media a window from 5 to 7pm for interviews. Some called me, others contacted Dave and Chris from Orlando or Meghan from Fusion PR. These calls added a little stress to all the last minute tasks that had to be accomplished.

My cold was worse and I tried resting when everything was accomplished. That helped a little and I got up feeling better. We had a photo session lined up for 2:30pm for the local newspaper. He arrived at 2pm and we weren't in uniform or ready, but he was patient. He got some great shots and with the plane out on the ramp, neighbors started coming over to wish us well.

---

1   030132z Zulu time, December 3rd, 1:32am, 5 hours ahead of Eastern Standard time, Dec. 2nd, 8:32 pm

We finally departed at 3:30pm, gassed up at Triangle FBO in Leesburg, who gave us a nice discount for our first leg fill-up, and arrived at MCO with ten minutes to spare. Friends were there, but no media, so we chatted for a while, then got to work as the different TV stations, photographers and journalists arrived. It was hectic for a while and VERY cold outside. Not at all a Florida evening. With my cold, I was chilled to the bone and shivering each time we had to go outside to the plane for pictures and interviews. Most of the interviews were done in the lobby of Galaxy Aviation, but we were LIVE on a local network newscast, unfortunately outside, with the plane behind us. I was hooked up with the mic and ear piece (just like the pros, it was kinda fun).

The person doing the organizing of the station sequences was speaking into my ear and telling me when we'd be on, I'd repeat for Carol and our local friends who were watching. There was a monitor, so we could see what was going on at the TV station, but when they were filming me I glanced at the monitor; it looked as if I was looking down, not at the camera. So, I tried to look at the blank camera when the announcer on the box was talking to me. I also noticed there was a delay between what I was saying and what was being broadcast; that was a little difficult at first.

Finally it ended and we ran inside to warm up. But, there were more cameras in the lobby. This continued for one and a half hours and was "fun" in a way. Actually it was very necessary to get our message across about ALS and why we are doing this flight. A number of the interviewers took the website information and will broadcast it. Hopefully the message will go beyond Orlando and Ocala.

I'd set the limit at 7pm, but we finally got "quiet time" at 7:20. I went to the pilot's lounge to lie down. Dave covered me with his blanket and I got half an hour of peace, stretching, and quiet. I felt better when I got up at 7:50. Wes and Sandy had arrived; big hugs all around. Dave wanted a few more pictures, then we headed for the plane. More hugs to everyone who had waited and helped us get to this moment.

I was in the left seat, Carol in the right. I did the checklist and started up; she called for clearances and asked if the tower had our Certification paperwork. Yes, they did, and "good luck" was the

Left to right: Debey, Tom, Carol, CarolAnn, Dave, Chris, Phil

reply. Clearance, ground, and tower all wished us the best. We told them we'd see them in eight days.

We were both starved. We hadn't eaten since a salad for lunch. So, we each had an apple and Power Crunch bar and some water. That hit the spot. I was exhausted and as soon as we were level and running on the rear tank, I took the first sleeping shift. Carol usually stays up later than I and it looked like this schedule would fit both of us.

Although I was exhausted and very comfortable with Carol in control, I couldn't sleep. Each time she moved, I could feel it. This was going to be a difficult trip if that continued. I finally just started an old meditation technique I'd learned long ago when living in France. That started to get me relaxed. Unfortunately, I was still cold. Every time I turned the heater up, a few minutes later Carol turned it back down. I knew it was stifling to her, but I was freezing and shivering. We finally reached a balance and I dozed and relaxed.

Carol's thoughts about the flight on departure:

Let's get out of here! I think CarolAnn and I had the same thing in mind – to just get going. After so much planning and anticipation, especially for her, we were grateful to finally push the throttle forward and fly.

It was beautiful with the stars and all of the airport lights. Taxiing out we received well wishes, and then we were cleared off to a grand adventure! The airplane did great, climbing smoothly up to altitude. The lights of Orlando twinkled below in a rainbow of colors, sending us off, yet beckoning us to come back again.

It was good to know that the woman beside me had so much more invested in this than I, is a mechanic, and that she was going to be an incredible mentor. It was good to know this airplane had been around the world before and thus knew the way. It was good to know that there would be personal friends greeting us in strange places with a smile when we got there. It was good to know we had the technology to be touched by another voice when it got lonely. It was good to know we had a professional staff of weather- and flight-planning experts to guide us through the air. It was good to know that so many people would be watching, tracking us, and sending positive energy. It was good to know that I wore angel epaulets and wings, in addition to the airman wings of a professional aviator. It was good to know that I had a special Lucky Lindy penny in my pocket that had never failed its owner. It was good to know we carried the hugs and support of friends and family that would bolster the wings of the plane and our spirits when things got tough. It was good to know the plane was protected with a Saint Christopher's medal blessed by the priest of a friend's parish. Gee, all we had to do was fly....for a long time!

Before two hours were up, I put my headset on and chatted a little. We filled out the hourly data sheet, Carol reminded me to do my stretching exercises and I felt pretty good. I prepare an email during the night:

It's just past midnight, EST, and I'm on watch. Carol took the first shift, my turn. I've done some position reports but we'll probably send everything out on the leg to Hawaii. We don't have the HF antenna out right now.

Almost 4 hours down and 11 to go. We had some unfavorable winds and will encounter more headwinds over TX and NM, but moving along well.

Air Traffic Control is passing the message down the line, so everyone is interested in our flight and web site.

Cold is still not good; but should be over it by tomorrow. Maybe Carol will have caught it by then.....

Looks like we'll be 45min late, not all that bad, considering the winds.

More next leg.

CA & CF

Carol's musings mid-flight:

Our flight plan was to initially take us over the Gulf, central Texas, past El Paso and Tucson, along the border and into San Diego. I was pretty excited because it looked like we would fly right over Spicewood at 2:30 am and a World Flight Watch Party on the ground was in the plans. There was talk of a flight joining up with us, a bonfire and chatter on the radio as we flew over. Well, the plan changed and instead we flew further north over Waco and Lampasas, disappointing everyone. I vowed to call on 122.8, the Spicewood frequency, when we got into the area anyway. I called and called, all the way from Waco to Lampasas, but everyone was sleeping, or so I thought. Turns out there were quite a few people watching us on FlightAware and listening on their handheld radios, but we just didn't hear each other. But, there was another contact opportunity to come.

A few days before leaving for the flight, Curtis, a FedEX pilot and Spicewood friend, contacted me by email and said that his schedule called for a flight from Memphis to Las Vegas on December 2nd. Undoubtedly, somewhere over west Texas we would be in the same airspace, and he would try to call us up. Well, there on Fort Worth Center, I heard FedEX 1440 asking if there was a N220FC on the frequency! Curtis and I chatted for about five minutes. I complained about the 35-knot headwinds and he complained about the 90-knot headwinds at FL340. He said he would let everyone back home know we were doing great and wished us luck and tailwinds the rest of the way.

We stayed at 4000 feet as long as possible early in the flight, to avoid the stronger headwinds at higher altitudes and for a while, as we got further west, it was pretty toasty, quite a change from our cold departure in FL. Once we climbed to 11,000 it was chilly and the heater came on again. We've been up here a while and using oxygen. With my cold, the cannula and oxygen didn't feel very good in my sore nose, so I start breathing it through my mouth; much more comfortable.

Overall, the night went pretty well. We both slept better on our second-sleep shift than the first, and we both feel pretty good this morning. The winds have been much stronger than forecast; for a while over Texas, we saw ground speeds between 89 and 96 knots. However, with good leaning, we'll still make it to San Diego without a fuel stop and only 45 minutes later than planned.

As morning arrives and we're flying over New Mexico, Carol asks if the mountains and deserts in New Mexico look like those in Africa. I said that the escarpments in Ethiopia will be steeper and I hadn't seen the western Sahara, so we'll see and learn about that at the same time....in a few days!

We'll land and able to stretch in two and a half hours. We're both ready for a good stretch. But, it's been a very successful first leg.

On the ground in San Diego

There are four cameras set up on the other side of the airport fence. Looks like the media has been informed. Jay Shower, an earth-rounder pilot/friend walks around the fence to welcome me then I reach over the fence to hug my brother, Richard. Carol heads to the bathroom and I take the first shift with the reporters.

As soon as we can, we start the refueling, Carol handles the oil and I work with the avgas guys. It's not a long leg to Hawaii, approximately 16 hours, but we want to do an intermediate over-gross

CarolAnn and her youngest brother, Richard,
share a quick laugh in San Diego.

Jay giving us a weather and departure briefing

takeoff. We'd already tested a takeoff at 110% gross from Orlando (during the test flight) and we'd be at 15% over gross from Hawaii. For this takeoff, although we didn't need all the avgas, we chose to be 13% over gross and right on the aft center of gravity to see how the airplane handled. Carol would be at the controls. We had 8000 feet of runway and the temperature was rising, but not hot. There was a slight breeze, but not a strong wind down the runway.

Jay gave me a full weather package and flight plan briefing. Normally the departure would have us head northwest to a VOR, then around the military airspace, then southwest. He'd talked with the powers that be and had approval for a straight out departure and through the military airspace, what a great help.

I hugged family and friends and waved our goodbyes to the media. We're off again after one hour and 35 minutes ground time.

—LEG TWO—

San Diego to Hawaii
(031954z², 11:54am local time)

Jay had received approval for us to talk with Beaver Control and to pass through their military airspace. After departure, we were turned over to Beaver and they radar vectored us through. What a great start. Unfortunately, winds were not favorable early on. The charts showed that they'd turn to tailwinds after a few hundred miles, which they did.

As Carol was sitting left seat and flying the first part of this leg, I started "playing" with all our electronic goodies. I reeled out the antenna so that we could communicate by HF radio to ATC and also send and receive HF email. I checked the email on the satellite phone and we had already received a satellite email from ground crew Flemming, in Switzerland:

---

2   031954z Zulu time, December 3rd, 7:54pm, 8 hours ahead of Pacific Standard time, Dec. 3rd, 11:54 am

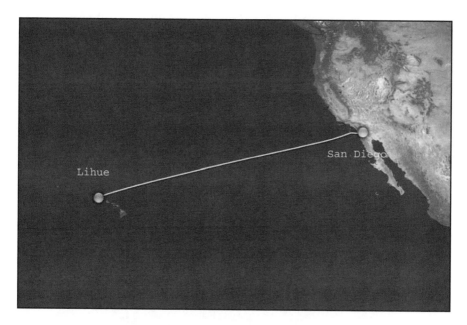

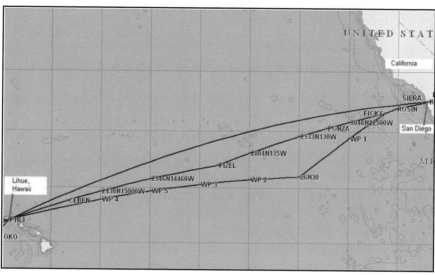

Top: Actual flight path by TracPlus Global Ltd.
Actual flight time, 16 hours 41 minutes
Bottom: Two planned routes depending on winds.
Top arc is the great circle distance between departure and arrival.
That's the distance used for the record calculations.

Good to see you off again, you should have better winds
on this leg, I saw when you hit that mountain wave east
of El Paso. Scary at night.

Flemming

He was referring to our speed slowing down near El Paso on the
previous leg. Flemming and the other ground crew had access to
the data on a high-power tracking device called TracPlus. They
could see everything we were doing, groundspeed, altitude, direction, and exact location over the ground, even zooming in to see
what was underneath us.

We sent updates to the web site during this leg:

Over the Pacific, The western sky is turning flame red
and it is reflecting on the top of the cowling. The Dash
for a Cure crew is cruising at 6,000' and it's smooth
while they listen to airliners make position reports to
San Francisco radio. We are well into the 2nd leg of the
trip after stopping at Brown Field, San Diego, this
morning. The flight from Orlando was long at 16:41 with
severe headwinds that kept the pilots calculating their
fuel reserves. The wind Gods are much more friendly on
the Pacific leg. Cruising over a cloud layer, you wouldn't
know there is ocean below, except that the pilots have
donned their life vests, have locator beacons handy as
well as the life raft. Once in Hawaii, we are looking
forward to some rest and the opportunity to reflect on
all of the help and support we have been given to
accomplish this flight. CF

I was also communicating with Bo, trying to find out about our
final permits and get the permit numbers for our flight plans:

Hello Bo -

We will arrive at Lihue Hawaii at midnight local time
tonight and head for Guam tomorrow. If you have sent
me any emails since Tuesday, I haven't received them.

If you have any new permit numbers, can you send
them to this address? I need to put Cambodia and the
new Thai number on the permit departing Guam on
Saturday morning.

Also, have you any news on India and Yemen?
Thank you, I'm tired, but all is going as planned.
CarolAnn

Carol's thoughts as we head over the Pacific:

*Oh boy, my first long over-water flight. Yea, I'd been down to
the Caribbean, over Lake Michigan and over the Gulf, but this
was serious blue water. I remembered one of the Caribbean
flights, a trip to the British Virgin Islands. It was a trip with
Bob.[3] During the 120 miles or so between the Dominican
Republic and Puerto Rico, I kept looking out the window and
remarking "Oh, darn, they're still there." Finally over land
again, I said "Well, good, they're gone now." Bob, now getting a
bit annoyed by my one-sided conversation, asked what I was
talking about. "Why, the group of sharks that have been
following us since Florida." I remarked. Hmmm....there are
sharks in the Pacific, too.*

*But, also remembering my shake-down flight across the
Gulf in October to visit CarolAnn, I was calm about what was
to come. It was on the Gulf flight, well beyond gliding distance
to land and out of sight of any ships, when your senses become
acutely aware of the airplane and the forces acting upon it, that
I felt this "hand" of support. It was literately holding up the
airplane. I could feel its pressure, its cradling of my plane as I
flew over the water. That's when I knew that all the aeronau-
tical engineers and Bernoulli didn't have the entire picture of
what makes a wing fly. I realized lift is also created by the positive energies of loved ones, present and past, and of the well
wishes and support of friends. We would be just fine.*

*Over the blue Pacific it was calm and peaceful. Underneath
us was a white blanket of cloud, and you would never know we
were over water except that we were wearing our life vests. A
few of the clouds reached our altitude of 6,000', but for the most
part it was very smooth. I remembered Jim, an airline pilot
friend, remarking that there is hardly ever any weather on the
way to Hawaii. All too soon after departing San Diego, the clear*

3   Bob was Carol's husband. He died of cancer in 2004.

blue space between the upper and lower layer of clouds turns a fiery red. We are treated to a spectacular sunset and are soon enveloped in a dark night, punctuated by twinkling stars.

Flying along with the autopilot engaged, I feel like I am in a cocoon, a capsule floating in space. A quick look outside reveals no horizon, no up or down and the air so smooth, I feel suspended. Even with the panel and instrument lights turned way low, the lights reflect yellow on the inside plastic windows. Looking outside is difficult at night with all of this reflection. To see the stars you have to put your face right up to the window and peer out into the blackness, but then you see them. Over the Pacific, the stars are spectacular!

Second email update to ALS website:

> 3 hrs to go. We just completed the fuel consumption calculations from San Diego to this point. We've used up the ferry tank and are running on mains. Total distance looks excellent for making the long legs to Guam, across Africa, and across the Atlantic. We are both tired but ecstatic; this was the confirmation we were waiting for. Couple more hours and we'll be in bed. Don't think we're going to head out early, as we're both exhausted. More tomorrow, CA

We alternated sleeping and flying throughout the evening and night. It was smooth and peaceful. As we approached Hawaii, we made VHF radio contact and I reeled in the tailing antenna. Several hours later Carol did an ILS 36 approach and smooth landing at Lihue, Hawaii at 2am. Interestingly, another plane had landed and another was preparing to depart. We were amazed at the activity at this time of night. We taxied to the public ramp, saw some signaling lights, followed the marshaler's direction to parking, and shut down.

We were greeted with leis and hugs from Roger Cable, Airport Support Network representative for AOPA and George Crabbe, Airport Manager. Within five minutes Roger had us loaded in the car and on the way to the hotel. We exchanged a few pleasantries, but I remember thinking how impolite we were being, not talking. We were just too exhausted to make much conversation. The hotel had already processed our information, gave us our keys and we were off to bed. We agreed to call Roger, or he'd stop by at 10am to pick us up.

I slept solidly, but woke up to the sound of chairs being dragged across the floor. My room was next to the breakfast eating area and food was being prepared. I felt pretty good with about five hours sleep, and realized that I wouldn't get any more peace and quiet, so decided to get up. Ahhhh, the shower was bliss. It rejuvenated my whole body... and I'd joked, prior to the trip, about not having the opportunity or need for a shower for seven days; what a mistake. This was great.

I don't know why emotions are so close to the surface this morning; maybe due to the stress of two days of flying. Anyway, I'm lying on the bed, thinking of my mother, and crying. Her life wasn't for nothing, she accomplished a lot, and I'm continuing her legacy by doing this trip in her memory to raise money to combat this terrible disease.

I called Universal Weather for the winds across the Pacific to Guam. They knew our route and Mike gave me the wind speed and directions at various latitudes and longitudes. The northern route would have headwinds for the first third of the leg. We'd never make 3231 nautical miles with those winds. However, if we headed southwest initially, then turned further west, we'd have tailwinds the whole trip. I revised our flight plan.

The schedule had been to call Chip and Jan Gulden once airborne off Lihue on our way. However, with the delayed arrival and departure, that wasn't going to work, so I called them an hour early from the hotel. Chip has had ALS for seven years and is bedridden. However, he is the most uplifting and positive person and a joy to meet and chat with. Jan answered and soon they were both on the speaker phone. I told them how the trip had gone so far and how welcoming the reception had been in San Diego and Hawaii. They said that they were following it on the web site and wished us well. I said, "This flight's for you, Chip." They mentioned that Chip's sister, Cheryl, would be in Orlando for our return. We didn't have a great connection through the satellite phone and got cut off, but not before lots of best wishes on both sides.

During a quick cup of coffee and croissant, I mentioned the call to Carol. She started crying. I said that I had already cried about my mom that morning. Obviously emotions were running high for both of us.

Carol's thoughts in the morning:

Rolling over in bed, I look at my surroundings and can't believe it. I'm in Hawaii! How on earth did I get here? Oh yea, I flew for 16 hours in a cramped and tiny space without any kind of in-flight catering or potty, never mind a few extra engines and I'm about to do it again, only for a longer time. Such were my thoughts as I padded to the bathroom pinching myself to know that it was real. On the way there, I saw a note on the floor. CarolAnn was already up and busy, and here I was, sleepy and somewhat irritable in paradise.

Things always work out and sometime lead to defining, bonding moments. CarolAnn is moving lightening fast this morning. Coffee. She has had some of that wonderful Hawaiian Kona coffee and is jazzed. She asks me to call Roger, our most wonderful contact, driver, aviator, and helper, to pick us up, but I can't! We got in too late last night to give a credit card to have my room phone activated! Aghhhh! So, I'll have to head downstairs to the desk to do it, I'm thinking, while putting on my shoes and zipping up my flight suit.

CarolAnn and I meet in the area on the 5th floor, the VIP floor, past where breakfast is served and we zip downstairs to get going. I feel like I'm being dragged around, totally useless and an idiot. How can I tell her this without looking totally useless and like an idiot? "CarolAnn, I'm sorry, but you are zipping around and I'm pretty slow this morning and a little grumpy. That will change when I wake up some more and get some coffee and food." That did it! She stopped in her tracks, looked at me and remarked that it was a really good thing that we were on somewhat different schedules. After all, she had been so tired and not feeling well last night with her cold, while I was able to rest adequately to be prepared to execute a nice ILS approach and land the plane.

While we waited for Roger, we went back upstairs for me to have some coffee and food, and CarolAnn decided to have a little more too. Yummm. Toast and fruit, fresh pineapple and good Hawaiian coffee! While we sat, she updated me on what she was up to, the flight plan, fueling and the weather. In addition she told me about a telephone call that she had with a friend who has ALS. She remarked that she wasn't sure that he would live long enough to see this world-flight attempt, but he had, and she had just talked to him. That did it for me. With my emotions so close to the surface, the big reason for all of this expense, effort, and involvement came crashing in on me. Thinking of my cousin Hal and all that he and his family have endured with this awful disease, and now this person, I began to cry and so did CarolAnn. We looked at each other and became a crew at a much deeper level.

We were MUCH chattier with Roger on our return to the airport. He was born into a flying family that ran Cable Airport in California; he'd flown all his life and he and his wife had settled in Lihue on the island of Kauai as being the most beautiful place they'd found in all their travels. We sure agreed it was beautiful and would both like to return and spend some time visiting the island.

The Air Services Hawaii people were efficient with weather, re-fueling and anything we needed. The Kauai Visitors Bureau and Sue Kanoho were most gracious having already provided the accommodation, they presented us with chocolates, macadamia nuts and a bag of Hawaiian goodies along with multiple checks of donations to ALS. What a presentation. We thanked them profusely, but had to be off. With a few more hugs and waves, we donned our life vests and entered the cabin again.

George Crabbe, Carol, Sue Kanoho, CarolAnn, and Roger Cable in Lihue, Hawaii

—LEG THREE—

Lihue, Hawaii to Guam
(042124z[4], 11:24am local time)

This was the BIG one, 15% over gross and a 6000 foot runway. Based on all the previous calculations, it would be well within our ability. The temperature was rising, but only about 26 C. The wind was right down the runway and when we got to the end, we saw it was a crowned runway. After 2000 feet, the runway dropped down towards the ocean. The takeoff was a "breeze" as the runway dropped away and we gathered speed, the plane just started floating. Not a great climb rate, but the ocean passed beneath us and we did a slow climbing turn to the southwest.

After reaching our cruise altitude of 6000 feet, we set the valves to use the fuel from the rear ferry tank, and settled in to our routine again.

---

4   042124z Zulu time, December 4th, 9:24pm, 10 hours ahead of Hawaii Std time, December 4th, 11:24 am

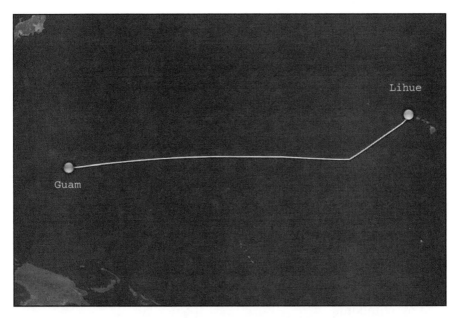

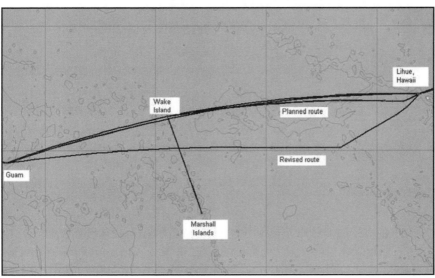

Top: Actual flight path by TracPlus Global Ltd.
Actual flight time, 23 hours
Bottom: Two planned routes depending on winds.
Line between Wake Island and the Marshall Islands shows
the location of our alternate airport

Early in this third leg, we received a satellite email from Suzanne at Universal Weather:

> "Hi! We're tracking you on SPOT. You must be deviating from the route to take advantage of the great winds? :)"
>
> Suzanne

She is right. I'd originally planned to fly the track on the Pacific chart from Lihue to Guam. It follows the great circle route and goes right over Wake Island. When the wind charts arrived in the morning, it showed that we'd have headwinds for the first third or 1000 miles of this leg. That wouldn't get us there. If we headed further south, then west, we'd get better tailwinds. That was the track we filed and were following. It was great to know they were following us and watching us that closely.

I sent an email to Doc on the carbon monoxide numbers we'd had on climbouts:

> Climbout from SDM at 3000' 30, 3600' 34 3700' 40.
>
> Level off COHb 1.1%. After 2 hrs, .7%, after 4 hrs .3%. Then 0.
>
> This morning we did a step climb, max 30, mostly 11 and 12.
>
> Level off COHb .4%, after 2 hours, .3%
>
> Are we still alive?
>
> Guam in 19 hours.
>
> Thank for your help,
>
> CarolAnn

These were the parts per million carbon monoxide, CO, count at various altitudes during our climb. Then, the measuring device calculates the carboxyhemoglobin percentage. That's what had Doc worried and what he most interested in. I gave him the reduction in percentage over time, so he could see how it diminished in our blood.

Carol's impressions at the start of this leg:

It was a breath-taking takeoff. With the down sloping black runway, the blue water beyond, puffy white clouds and the green mountains off to the side, the Mooney glided seemingly without effort into the air. This was the beginning of the leg I was personally most concerned with. For the next hour or so, as I was wedged into the seat, I gazed out the window, paying close attention to the patterns of the waves.

Observing water swells and patterns are important for survival. I learned this at an FAA survival school that I attended in November in preparation for this trip. Ditching parallel and on top of the primary swell is vital in minimizing the impact of touch down on the water in an airplane. Now looking out the window I could vividly see what the instructor was talking about. I imagined the whole ditching process. As with any emergency maneuver, flying the airplane is first. It is slowed for ditching to an air speed between best glide and stall. Interestingly, best glide resulting in the furthest distance is not the target speed since it doesn't matter where you land because it's going to be in the water.

What really needs to happen is the airplane needs to be slowed as much as possible upon touchdown. The next important thing is to get the life raft and emergency equipment ready and to prop open the door. CarolAnn and I had discussed this procedure and decided the Mooney would be landed with the landing gear and the flaps up. Upon touchdown with the primary swells, the raft gets thrown out while tethered to the airplane, inflated and we follow after inflating our life vests as quickly as possible with the personal GPS locator beacon and SAT phone. One of the films in training I saw was an actual ditching of an airplane into the water. It was a Mooney! Since I saw that a ditching had already been done in a Mooney successfully, I decided we really didn't need to do that.

Amazingly, the chances of survival, even in the middle of the ocean, are about 82% if you get into the raft. So, at survival school I practiced with an inflated life vest in the pool swimming to a raft, righting it and climbing into it. In addition, we practiced the procedure of getting out of an airplane cockpit while upside down and underwater. During this practice, I experienced a moment of panic when I couldn't find the latch for my seatbelt. I had to calm my thinking, work through the problem and escape, because I knew my life depended upon it! If this is what we have to do at some moment, we're getting into our raft.

We've been flying now for a while and its time for me to de-clutter my area. Our raft, which I affectionately dubbed the "Baby" is a 31-pound, yellow and orange vinyl package, 11"x 7"x 22" with straps, that has to be moved from alongside of the copilot's legs to its spot behind the pilot and under the ferry tanks. In this process of shifting things around, every movement requires thought, effort and patience. Moving Baby is a three-step process taking about ten minutes of time. Of course, I have to pat and praise Baby, making sure there is no reason for it to wake up and want to be used while putting it into its bed.

Step one was to position myself way to the left with the seat fully back so I could slide the raft up along the side of the fuselage, past the HF wire reel, twisting it to avoid bumping the yoke until it's sitting on my lap. This is a good time to give it a hug, telling it that it will soon be in its bed and can just sleep the rest of the trip. Step two is to have the pilot lean as far forward as she can with all of the various bags on her lap, pushing her seatback forward so I could lift Baby into the space between us, being careful not to hit the ferry tank fuel selector valve while placing Baby on the floor behind her seat. Whew, time for another rest and more cooing praise for our raft. The final step was to rotate the raft from a vertical to a horizontal position, slide it along the floor to wedge it under the shelf built for the ferry tanks. Tucked in, Baby got its final strokes and wishes for a good sleep, and I rested grateful that was completed for another leg. Six legs of the world flight required this process.

I sent an update to the website:

> Our stop in Lihue, Hawaii was fantastic. There was a newspaper article the day before our arrival. Most donations were made on line, but they gave us three hundred dollars in additional donations to ALS-TDI. The bed rest was exactly what we needed. Roger drove two zombies who said next to nothing to the hotel and picked up two excited pilots the next morning. Roger coordinated everything and gave us lots of fruit for this leg. We had coffee in the morning, exactly what the doctor ordered. We've been underway for 4 hours now. The computer is still saying 19 hours to go; but we should pick up tailwinds as we head south and turn more westerly. After the first two legs, we're thinking seriously about stopping overnight in Djibouti and Cape Verde. That will change our overall schedule, but keep fatigue at bay. Will keep everyone advised.
>
> Thank you all for your support.
>
> CarolAnn and Carol

After several more hours I wrote on my kneeboard:

> What's tough is watching the sun go down, beautiful sunsets, after almost nine hours of flying, feeling slightly tired and knowing that we still have 14 hours to go to Guam. That's mentally and physically very difficult.

Carol's impressions:

> *Night falls and CarolAnn and I fall into a loose routine of a few hours on and a few hours off. We are almost halfway to Guam and we calculate our fuel flow and reserves. CarolAnn and I discuss deviation options briefly before she decides to take some sleep time. Just before she removes her headset she says, "If you decide to deviate, wake me up." Yikes! This is a really long flight leg, with a point of no return that has to be determined well in advance because once we are past that point, the only option is water. This really stresses me out. It's a calculation I have to consider and look at hard, especially if something like fuel flow or winds change. For the next two hours I'm thinking about the math involved in this decision. If we go past Wake Island or the*

Marshall Islands, our alternate, we'll have so much fuel, but will be faced with headwinds if we turn back. So to what point can we go and still have a good reserve? What reserve am I comfortable with landing in Guam or the Marshall Islands? What's the weather in Guam? Will we have to do an approach? Admittedly, I wasn't able to come up with a definitive answer, other than at each time I calculated the anticipated fuel landing in Guam, we would have two hours still in the tanks. I was comfortable with this reserve and told CarolAnn we would make Guam at about 6:30 in the morning.

Still alternating sleeping and flying responsibilities, we finally got over the halfway point. The timers showed 11 hours to go and 12 hours and 15 minutes completed. Based on winds, the readouts changed slightly, but it was looking like a 23-hour leg.

We're feeling tired. After half a night in a hotel in Lihue, we recovered a bit, but it's enough to tell us that we won't be able to continue across Africa without a stop. I email Universal Weather and ask them to book us a hotel in Djibouti for the night we arrive, December 8th. As we had planned to fly across Africa between December 8th and 9th, the permits would still be good for the 9th. But, that would be the limit. If anything went wrong, we'd have to get new permits.

The laptop is using battery, not ship's power. It's halfway down before I notice it. We started checking the wiring and systems. Everything else is working.... Looking at the cigarette lighter adapter, we finally found that the fuse was blown. I sent an HF email to Elsie, Carol's contact in Guam. I explain about the cigarette lighter and she responds that she'll get one. Super. We don't do many updates during the rest of the trip. We keep enough battery power in case we need to get emails out. Our ETA is 6am. If we get four hours in a hotel, we could plan to depart about 1pm.

I look at our arrival and departure log to this point, with two legs completed. We arrived at our first stop 45 minutes late and departed one hour late. We arrived in Hawaii two hours late and departed two hours later than planned. At this rate and with our current leg underway, we'll probably arrive in Thailand at 6am. I get an email off to Norm to advise them of the slight delay and new arrival time. No sense having everyone stay up all night waiting for us.

When it comes time to change from the rear tank, we're both awake and watching the fuel pressure guage. Sometimes it drops quickly and the engine coughs before we catch it. Sometimes we catch it first. This time the engine coughed first. We hit the boost pump and switched tanks, but it continued coughing — it took longer than usual to pickup and run normally. We both had our hearts in our mouths. Finally it ran smoothly. We noted the time and did our calculations. We would have two hours fuel remaining upon landing in Guam. GREAT.

Carol has some level of frustration with the HF radio communication. Every hour we are to report our position, altitude, and estimated position for the next hour. Sometimes the communication is smooth and clear, at other times it's very difficult to hear the controller and to understand what he's saying. I explain that this will become more difficult with different accents as we continue. Right now, with US controllers, it's not too bad.

I'd spoken with Chris on Wake Island prior to departure and told him we'd call when passing over. With us being on a southern route, we didn't pass over the island, so I called him on the satellite phone. He had just gone off duty an hour ago. Bummer, but I spoke with Lou. Chris had told him about our flight and they'd looked at our web site. Then he said something amazing; what a coincidence. Chris had met Jerry Mock on Wake Island when she was on her record-setting flight around the world in 1964. She was the first woman to fly across both the Pacific and Atlantic Oceans and around the world. She set numerous speed records later in her flying career. Wow. If we'd been on the northern route, I think I'd have asked for permission to land so that we could meet Chris and Lou on our record-setting flight.

Carol's notations on crossing the International dateline:

A monumental occasion has occurred! We toast it with the macadamia nuts we took along from Hawaii, not having champagne, chocolate or any other celebratory item with which to ritualize this event over the Pacific. We have crossed the International Date Line! From one moment to the next we are a day older and will begin the process of becoming younger

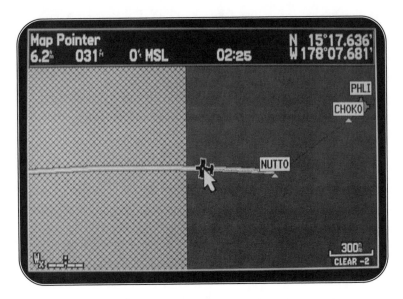

GPS view of crossing the International Date Line

again. In addition, we would be entering the eastern hemi-
sphere until we would be just beyond Niamey, our alternate
Africa stop, where we would cross 0° longitude and be back in
the western hemisphere. In general, calculating local times was
a mind bending process as we traveled, especially when we
were tired. Thankfully, a lot of this had been done before we
left, and CarolAnn had a great chart to consult. We laughed at
the handheld Garmin GPS when I zoomed out to see the entire
route between Hawaii and Guam. West of the International
Dateline it changed color and pattern. I remarked "Hey, look at
this! We are going to fly off the edge of the earth!" Fortunately,
the Garmin changed back to its ocean blue after the dateline,
and we did not fly off the edge but, unfortunately, I didn't have
any less grey hair.

I woke up to a black sky. The moon had set, but there were
millions of stars out and Orion was just above us. Less than six
hours to go. Carol will sleep as I take over the controls and radio.
I'll be flying pilot for two hours, and then we'll switch again.

The sun came up behind us with scattered clouds below. Approach advised us that there was moderate rain between Guam and us, but we'd be able to get around behind it. We started descending and passing between buildups. We could see the island, then the airport. A full approach would have taken us ten miles further to the southwest, so I opted for a visual approach and they cleared us immediately. There were a few showers and winds were howling down the runway at 17 knots gusting to 28.

The ground crew guided us to just in front of a big hangar. Photographers and journalists were waiting. As we got out, we both felt the earth kept moving. It was like getting off a boat after time at sea. I held on to the plane or kept my arms out. Besides being stiff and achy, this was a new sensation. We were interviewed, photographed, and presented with shell leis. We finally pulled the Mooney into the hangar, just as a rain shower hit. One of the photographers got a fantastic photo of the Mooney with a vivid rainbow behind.

Chuck loaded us in his car and whisked us off to the nearby Days Inn. We ordered lunch to be delivered by noon and headed off to bed. With ground support like this, we'd be able to maximize our sleep time and minimize hassle and paperwork time.

It was a short but solid four hours. As I lay down on the bed, I heard a big jet depart and thought, *Oh, I'll never sleep though that.* The next thing I knew it was four hours later and I awoke in the same position — I don't think I moved. After a shower and checking satellite phone messages, I headed out to find our food which had been ordered for noon delivery. Carol appeared out of her room at the same time!! We decided to eat together and discuss the day's plans. I was actually feeling great, looked like my cold was finally over. Let's just hope that Carol hasn't caught it.

Chuck picked us up at 12:30 and we headed to the airport. Carol's friend's friend Gary was there along with a TV crew. We did a quick interview along with more pictures.

Carol's friends and contacts:

Now, I hoped to see Gary, the boom operator for my retired Air Force pilot friend Bill. Bill and Gary served together in Vietnam

Roseminda, CarolAnn, Carol, Chuck

and had stayed in touch. Here would be another example of a friendly face greeting us at a far away place. In addition, Gary got us in touch with Tim, Guam International's ATC manager, who paved the way for our arrival, landing and departure. This world flight is indeed an example of aviation networking at its best.

Looking forward to a little horizontal sleep, shower and maybe some real food, we landed Guam and were treated royally. The Days Inn near the airport was to be our rest stop for a few hours as we were planning on departing again about 1pm. Ahhh, sleep. I almost dozed off and remembered to call Gary! I invited him to please come see us off and thanked him for his efforts on our behalf.

Gary and his wife Kay greeted us at the entrance to the hangar. It was just incredible to make this connection halfway around the world. What a marvelous time we live in where communication is completed at the touch of a "Send" button.

Mel opening barrel number two.

After I got home to Spicewood, Bill told me a little about Gary and the way he took care of his pilots. No request was too great for Gary. One story was how Gary didn't let his pilots eat the normal rations, but instead brought a stove and cooked them steaks to order. I saw these qualities in the man who greeted me, and am privileged to have met him.

After cleaning up the plane we shook hands all around and hugged Chuck; what unexpected support and hospitality. We taxied out to the fuel station. I was a little surprised to see four barrels on a forklift truck with an electric pump attached to a ladder. Mel, the mechanic, started to explain that shipments of fuel had been delayed and their normal fuel tanker wouldn't be operational again for three more weeks. It took just over an hour, but we were ready to depart, with many thanks to Mel, Gene, and Satoru for helping.

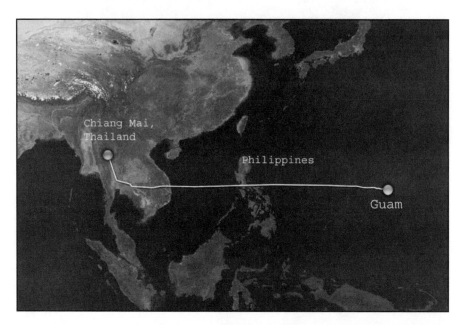

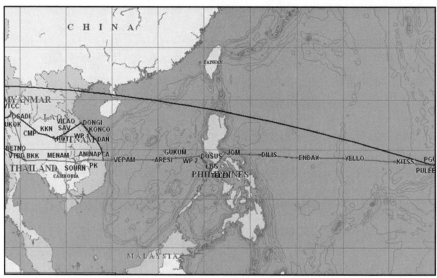

Top: Actual flight path by TracPlus Global Ltd.
Actual flight time, 20 hours 23 minutes
Bottom: Planned routes with optional routes over land.

—Leg Four—

Guam to Chiang Mai, Thailand
(060431z[5], 2:31pm local time Dec. 6th)

Carol taxis down the parallel runway, runs up on the taxiway, and we await the arrival of two jumbo jets. Then it's our turn. With 10,000 feet of runway, we climb slowly over the ocean and head west.

Carol's thoughts:

> *My leg as PIC again as we climbed into the airplane. We had to wait for our clearance to take off due to landing traffic; one of the aircraft was a Northwest Airlines 757. My late husband, Bob, was a captain for Northwest Airlines and had flown to Guam and Southeast Asia during the last part of his career. Departing, I didn't know this would be a very emotional flight.*

Soon after sitting in my seat I recognized a problem... I hadn't exercised during the ground stop. I had a super backache right in the middle on the left-hand side. I couldn't find a comfortable position, try as I might. I rubbed it, stretched, twisted, sat up straight, slouched, bent over, pulled my knees to my chest... this was going to be one tough leg. I certainly wouldn't forget to stretch during the next rest stop, big mistake, it was killing me. Carol had taken the time to stretch and said she was fine. Oh, I was sore.

We had 1300 miles from Guam to the Philippines then another 800 miles across the South China Sea to Vietnam, and the final 800 miles over Cambodia and Thailand to Chiang Mai. I set up the HF and sent out an update:

> Sorry for lack of updates yesterday. 23 hour flight, all went well, except lost charging for laptop. That resulted in no updates and no HF emails. We continued our critical emails through sat phone email. We received wx, winds and permit updates.

---

5   060431z Zulu time, December 6th, 4:31am, 10 hours behind Guam time, December 6th, 2:31pm

We alternated 2hr shifts sleeping/resting and being flying pilot. Both stayed relatively well rested and felt OK for approach and landing. We had the Panasonic video recorder on as we descended through and between the clouds and did a visual to runway 6R at Guam. We received a warm welcome (same as Hawaii), moved the Mooney into the hangar, and were driven to the hotel.

To stay on time for the permit countries, we opted for 4 hrs sleep, a quick snack, and back to the airport for fueling, TV interviews, and takeoff.

The refueling is a story in itself as they hadn't received their normal shipments and had to refuel us from 55gal drums!! Pics and description in the upcoming book, coming out soon!!

Nice departure over blue waters and around puffy little rain clouds. Enjoying a 14 knot tailwind at this point, our flight time could be shorter than the planned 19 hours.

More later; thanks for all your support.

BTW, the last permit came through yesterday while flying. Bo obtained the India permit number; we were ecstatic. I think we celebrated with macadamia nuts given to us in Lihue.

Feeling GREAT,

CarolAnn and Carol

We're at 14,000 feet flying over the Philippines at night, using oxygen. There are headwinds and our groundspeed is 126 knots. What's worse is we know there are good tailwinds below and the controller won't let us down. Finally, on the west side of the Philippines, we descend to 10,000 and get some improvement. Looks like the rest of the trip will be at this altitude. East of the Philippines we had had rain and turbulence; there were scattered clouds over the city and we saw the lights. West of the city everything cleared up and the moon came out to greet us again tonight.

At the waypoint VEPAM, we cross the Philippines airspace and Hochiminh FIR boundary (Ho Chi Minh). We're now in Vietnamese airspace. Nothing changes, we continue communicating our position and altitude and they read back our position. Over Vietnam, Cambodia and Thailand we can see town and city lights below the clouds. It's still night and we can't see any relief, but I believe there are some hills down there; most of the mountainous area is in Vietnam. We have light turbulence, but not much.

Carol's thoughts:

Part of the success in a flight like this is preparation. CarolAnn had spent a huge amount of time flight planning, researching weather and winds, getting the plane ready, coordinating fuel at the various stops and making arrangements for permits in addition to looking back at her previous experience traveling around the world.

I had the opportunity in 2007 to fly as part of a crew in a small jet from San Antonio to Southampton, England. To prepare for that trip I reviewed information in the FAA Advisory Circular 91-70. It's a really lengthy document covering oceanic operations describing radio procedures, altitudes to fly, position reports, airspace control, safety, ditching, equipment requirements and many more topics. For this world trip I reviewed AC 91-70 again. With position reporting I remembered that occasionally, particularly when traveling at low altitudes like we would be doing, it would be necessary to relay your report to the appropriate radio station via an airliner. I had to do some relaying through an airliner on my trip to Florida over the Gulf of Mexico in October. Cool! I thought. Wouldn't it be neat if I had to relay a position report through Northwest Airlines somewhere over Southeast Asia? And thinking further, wouldn't it be extraordinary if someone on that NWA crew knew Bob? This was a wild dream but it stayed in the back of my mind.

Departing Guam there were a few rain showers and buildups to fly around. The sunset was grand as we picked our way around the clouds. Satellite images had shown that there may be some rain east of the Philippines and there was. At night we flew through them somewhat disturbing our rest, but we really tried to maintain a schedule of duty on and duty off. Flying through one of the bumpier showers tested our crew coordination and trust. I was jolted awake by the rocking of wings and the sound of rain. Peering over the blanket, I thought I had better help with this since I'm in the left seat. I placed my hands on the yoke. CarolAnn disengaged her control and, after a while, got the computer out to do other work. When I was ready to go back to sleep, she said, "Let's talk about this later."

When day came and we were both alert, the subject of control was reviewed. We decided that if the pilot flying needed help from the snoozing crew, we would wake them up. However, if the non-flying left-seat pilot saw something threatening they would place their hands on the yoke, verbalize the issue and take control. This discussion between us was so beneficial because it cleared up issues of responsibility and defined definitively how we would act. It also lead to better rest periods because I trusted her skills and I was confident CarolAnn would call for my help when she needed it. I could really relax.

Somewhere over the Philippines, I took out my iPod that was loaded with music and a few movies like "Airplane", "Forever Young", The American Aviator", and The Incredibles". I really wanted to see some of these movies again thinking that we would be laughing our way across the Pacific. Ha Ha. The fifteen minutes I put the earbuds in to impatiently listen to a few songs was about all I could handle, never mind sitting there to watch a movie! It was much more interesting and necessary to complete our hourly reports monitoring the airplane, update the ALS website on our location and status, communicate via SAT phone to our ground crews, maintain position reports and HF communication, anticipate the ferry tank running dry, rest, eat, scribble down some notes, and for some short snatches of time, look out the window and think about where we were! We were too busy for entertainment.

For me, it was now getting really interesting to listen and talk on the HF radio. Accents were no longer American and the names of the radio stations we were calling were beginning to sound exotic, like Manila Radio, Ho Chi Minh Radio, Kolkata Radio and Phnom Penh Control. The airline companies were changing too. Heard were Cathay Pacific, Philippine Airlines, Thai Airways, Air Asia, Air China, and Singapore Airlines mixed together with an occasional Delta, United and Northwest. But, I was also getting frustrated.

Talking on the HF radio is a formal process. There is no idle chit-chat because the conveying of aircraft position is very serious and many times the connections are tenuous and difficult to hear. It's really important that your position be reported accurately and in a timely manner. Air traffic control utilizes the reports to monitor traffic flow, adherence to clearances and as an opportunity for aircraft to check in to report that operations are normal. Most significantly, it is from these reports that search and rescue personnel will start looking for a tiny raft floating in a big ocean. When a position is reported, the radio station always repeats it back for accuracy and they will question you if something is not right. I thought of it like a serious game of Telephone, especially when the report had to be relayed via airliner. You can hear everything, but can't communicate directly. Sometimes it takes three tries to get it right. With the picture of us floating in the ocean, it could take four.

"Ho Chi Minh Radio, Ho Chi Minh Radio, N220FC, Position". "Ho Chi Minh Radio, Ho Chi Minh Radio" N220FC, Position". Nothing. I couldn't get them on either the primary or the secondary HF frequency. There's nothing to do but note the reporting point we were over and the time, the estimated time for the following point and the one after that, wait and try again. I was into a multiple cycle of this over the South China Sea when I heard "Northwest 19, this is Ho Chi Minh Radio....see if you can raise a N220FC on the frequency". Oh good! We will be able to relay our position so they could find us if the engine quit. I was relieved. Then it struck me. Oh, this is Northwest Airlines! I wonder if it is a 747-400, Bob's aircraft. Too busy to muse anymore, NWA 19 called us and requested our position report to be relayed to Ho Chi Minh Radio. I gave them the report which I noted was accurately transmitted. With the minutest hesitation and ignoring protocol because this was too important, I keyed the mike, said "Thank you, Northwest 19, for the relay and do any of your crew members know Bob Foy?" I held my breath thinking there was no way that anyone would. After all, it was summer of 2003 the last time he flew. In 15 seconds the answer came back that, yes, one of the crew members remembered Bob.

Oh, my gosh! Is there not someone, some spirit, some energy, some entity that guides, directs or creates ones point of being to be at a certain time and space? I don't know what to call this. Coincidence? Luck? This is too much and in my mind another example of the positive energy that surrounds this flight. I told the NWA crew who I was and what I was doing. NWA Flight 19 was en route to Singapore. The crew would be wishing us well while raising a glass of beer to Bob and me when they got on the ground during their "debriefing". As I was shaking my head and absorbing what had just happened, I heard "N220FC, this is NWA 19, come up on 123.45", the air-to-air frequency. I did and got to talk briefly to Joe, a NWA sales manager and personal friend of Bob's. Amazing! I knew there would be laughter and Bob stories told that night, and I found out later there were a lot of Bob's NWA colleagues tracking CarolAnn and me around the world.

Not too much can top this, I thought. Later, after things had quieted down and positive contact had been made with the controllers, things were more relaxed and it was my time to rest. It's funny the thoughts that pop into your head. I had a conversation with my late husband that brought tears, wonder, resolve, joy, and peace. Not too many hours later, I landed the plane in Chiang Mai and he was gone.

We pass into Thailand and head northwest, then north. We report to Bangkok air traffic control. Then the next ATC area has a difficult name, Phitsanulok. We both laugh as we can't pronounce it. Luckily, when Bangkok approach hands us over, they call it PSL, Papa Sierra Lima approach, that's the VOR identifier for the airport. We are both relieved.

After PSL we're handed over to Chiang Mai. It's morning and there's a heavy haze. The ATIS is saying 3000 meters visibility. It's almost a straight in ILS approach and I see the runway several miles out. We land after 20 hours and 23 minutes of flying and follow the taxi instructions to station 14. We're parked next door to an Air Asia airliner.

There are multiple crews to meet us. Bo, the Nok station manager (subsidiary of Thai Airways International), and several

Top: CarolAnn, Bo, and Carol
Above: Our Thai helpers, Yui and Yui

helpers take care of all the paperwork with customs, passport info, and handle the landing and parking paperwork. The mechanics from SGA are ready to take the cowling off and start on the maintenance work. I explain that I'd like to be there with them, but am tired and need sleep. We set 1pm to get together for the maintenance session. I was sorry to put them off, they looked so enthusiastic about starting the work.

Bo and crew got us through the immigration formalities, into a bus and to the hotel within 30 minutes. We signed in and heads hit the pillows. Unfortunately, a housekeeping person knocked on the door two hours later. I couldn't get to sleep after that. I tossed and turned for a while and gave up. Actually I noticed that my ribs hurt.

Each time I tried to take a full breath, the bottom third of the left rib cage had a dull pain. Enough to stop me taking a full breath. I wondered what was going on.

Finally I got up and did some stretching exercises; that felt better. When Carol woke up, I said I'd take a shower then go find an Internet connection and check weather. She appeared half an hour later; I showed her the winds across India....not favorable. Actually, not doable at 10,000 feet. We'd definitely have to stop in India if we ran into those winds. Possible at 5000 feet, but certainly not the tail-winds we wanted.

Bo arrived, we thanked the hotel manager, took pictures, and headed back to the airport. He and his efficient crew got us through immigration again; we paid the landing and parking fees and were escorted to the plane. Bo is a nickname for Tadthai. He said in English it means "kick someone." I wondered what he was like as a kid. He certainly is a helpful gentleman now!

The SGA folks were ready and waiting. Screwdrivers came out and they started taking the cowling off. Before I had time to get the oil hose from the rear of the plane, they already had one connected and were pouring the used oil into a bucket. As another mechanic is loosening the oil filter, I pulled two "special tools" from the plane, a long piece of bent aluminum for the oil to drain outside the cowling instead of down the firewall and a short 1" wrench that fits better on the oil filter. In the Mooney's confined engine space, special tools are helpful for maintenance. They all nodded their heads as they understood immediately the usefulness of the tools. I cleaned the K&N air filter as the oil change was underway.

After that, we started taking out the spark plugs. I checked each one and rotated them top to bottom and between cylinders. They inserted them and tightened them. Thankfully, they had a torque wrench. In no time, that job was complete. Last job was checking the magneto timing. I pulled out my magneto timer to oohs and ahhs from the mechanics. Obviously they didn't expect me to carry one of those on my trip; another "special tool." I connected the leads, turned the prop to the correct position and turned on the ignition. They knew to be careful at this point and stepped back. I tapped the propeller to bring it slowly to the correct position. Behind me, one of the mechanics is saying, "tap, tap, tap" with each

CarolAnn and Thai mechanics giving a hand

movement I make. Finally the light goes on and I check the rotation position, 22 degrees. I tap once more and the second light goes on, 21 degrees. Perfect, well almost. They were 21 and 20 when we departed. Art said I didn't have to touch them if they were less than 23 degrees. I'm elated, we're good to go.

After cleaning everything up, I do a test run. Everything looks and sounds good. The mechanics give the engine a thorough check, no oil leaking, nothing looks out of place. We're ready to re-cowl.

During this time, Carol's been busy with food, water, coffee — thanks a million, I needed that. After working in the sun, I'm pretty beat and swallow a whole bottle of water. She's cleaned up the cockpit, prepared the paperwork and charts, filed the flight plan, and we're almost ready to go.

The fuel truck shows up. We'd used an ATM in the terminal to get enough Thai Baht to cover this cost. We weren't going to fuel to 15% over gross as the airport is at 1000 foot elevation and it's warm, 26 C. Also, we need to climb to 7000 feet over mountains on departure. The leg isn't that long, but the winds aren't favorable, so I'd like to take on more fuel, but the other considerations take precedence. We can't climb to IFR altitudes to cross the mountains, so Carol has filed a VFR/IFR flight plan. We'll depart VFR, climb over the mountains visually, maintaining separation from terrain, then, over the Bay of Bengal, we'll pick up our IFR clearance.

After only two hours of sleep and three hours of maintenance on the ramp, I'm tired as we head out and still worried about the two wind charts we saw earlier today. Both showed westerly winds across the Indian Ocean, stronger on west side as we would head off the coast from Mumbai to Salalah, Oman; they forecast 25 knots at 270 degrees, at 10,000 feet. If that's what we're up against, we won't make it.

With a few more pictures and lots more hugs, we're buckled up and taxiing out.

Carol's thoughts on Chiang Mai:

How lovely this place is! We have been greeted warmly by the most pleasant people. We are definitely someplace else, with colorful paper lanterns hanging from the ceiling in the main terminal and every sign a delightful work of fanciful art. I love the Thai lettering with all of the curliques, colors and unrecognizable, exotic spellings. After paying our airport fees and gathering our belongings for a short sleep, we are off in a van to the hotel. As a landscape architect I'm impressed with the gardens and the plantings along the route. Amazingly, a median barrier is created by a series of steel supports placed about three feet apart to which is attached a large metal ring. In each ring is a 10-ft. pot of mums that are either yellow or orange so the effect for at least a half mile is a colorful strip of flowers that guides the traffic along the road. Elsewhere, the tropical foliage is well manicured, giving way to the many shops, colorful street stalls and intersections graced with cow statues adorned with flowers around their necks. A sign of good luck, I see some elephant statues as well. I spy two women also on a life adventure. They have giant backpacks, bandanas around their heads and are talking with animation to a shop keeper. Oh, I wish I could be younger and participate in such an adventure! Well, I guess I'm not that old, and I am participating in an adventure as we travel through the hustle and bustle.

The hotel of dark teak, white-washed walls and lush green tropical foliage is an oasis away from the busy street. I have to sleep. It's the middle of the day after much stimulation and it's hard to find rest. Also, although an absolutely lovely hotel, CarolAnn and I must share a room. There is slight tension to coordinate our personal needs and I will myself to sleep. More successful than CarolAnn, I wake last and quickly prepare for a shower.

Soap and water are most missed on this trip. In the middle of any flight leg, even though we have sanitizer and cleansing cloths, I'd give anything for soap and a basin of water just to wash my hands. Well, here is a beautiful basin, granite countertop and a fabulous shower with fluffy towels that I can't spend too much time enjoying. What stops me short to think about what I am doing and where I am, however, is when I lift my friend's gifted crucifix from around my neck and place it carefully on the countertop. I think about how charmed I am, how lucky I am to have so many people who care about me, and the many that are following this flight with hopes of success and excitement. Here I am, almost halfway around the world being supported by all of this positive energy. How could I not get home to them? How could I ever express my gratitude? How would I react when I saw them again? Would life be different? Would I be different? I had come to discover that I didn't have any reasons not to do this trip, but I had so very many reasons to go home.

Back at the airport we are busy preparing N220FC, dubbed "the little one" by the locals, for departure. Indeed, we are tiny parked amongst the large fuselages and wings of the airliners. CarolAnn is directing an entire maintenance crew and I take on the task of finding us some food and water which will be available in the terminal. But first I have to talk to CarolAnn's friend Norm about the terrain we are to travel over on the way out of Thailand. It's quite hazy; we can't climb to the minimum altitudes for IFR and must fly visually, so local knowledge of what we are to see is welcome. I am cautiously comfortable in these conditions of low visibility. Air racing in marginal VFR condi-

tions as well as numerous trips to the East Coast and Midwest where these conditions prevail has become the norm in my experience. It's been interesting to see and explore the different comfort levels between CarolAnn and me. Our experiences complement us as crew.

After the conversation, I am deposited by the van on the ramp side of the terminal doors to wait for my escort. I'm standing there looking around at the foreign, to me, airliners on the ramp and thinking about the colorful terminal decorations when I detect a smell. Hmmm. What is that odor? I look down and notice I am standing on a grate and see raw sewage flowing under my feet. OK. I'm in a different country, ventilation is required and good, here comes my escort into the terminal. Actually, I'd love to come back to Chiang Mai for a visit, staying at the same lovely hotel to enjoy the shower longer and getting to know these wonderful people.

— LEG FIVE —

Chiang Mai, Thailand to Salalah, Oman
(070900z[6], 4:00pm local time)

There's not much traffic, but what little there is decides to arrive as we're leaving. We have to wait about 15 minutes at the end of the runway for arriving traffic. Finally we're off...there's not much to see with the haze and approach is giving us radar vectors. They turn us west, where the mountains are, and a climb. We have all eyes peeled looking outside for peaks. There's one... one more over to the right.... Another over there. We're clear. Oh, looks like another range ahead. Finally we're up to 7000 feet and clear of the peaks. We both give out a sigh of relief.

---

6   070900z Zulu time, December 7th, 9:00am, 7 hours behind Thailand time, December 7th, 4:00pm

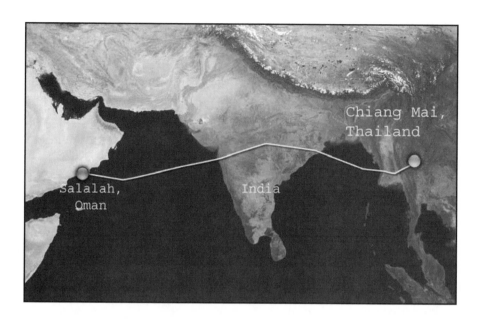

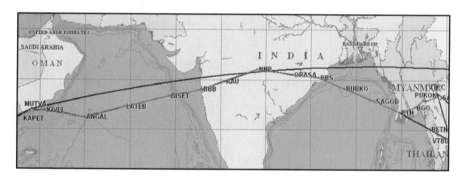

Top: Actual flight path by TracPlus Global Ltd.
Actual flight time, 20 hours
Bottom: Planned route. Most northerly point, Nagpur, India

We turn northwest and head over Myanmar's coast and site of the spring 2008 cyclone disaster. We can't see much but lots of water and low land. Any cyclone would have ripped right through there.

As we head out over the water, we hit headwinds right from the start. We're both concerned. Keep watching the groundspeed and total time to destination. We know we have 24-hours endurance, but strong head winds in the last several hundred miles could mean not making it. We have to make the decision over India, or within range of land, if we have to turn back.

The ground crews see that we're off and send their wind reports; we should be receiving a tailwind, NE light, but there. Instead we have 8- to10-knot headwinds and groundspeeds of 113 to 119 knots. We're pretty glum and I'm thinking of options. Early in the planning stage I'd looked at a technical halt in Nagpur, just to gas up and continue. That's my backup plan. If these don't subside, we'll need more fuel. We check with ATC and drop to 6000 feet; that helps a little, but not much.

I'm exhausted and take the first sleep shift. Actually, it's smooth and for the first time in the flight, I take my seat belt off and have an "ah ha" moment...I can breathe again. It was the seat belt, fastened over the life jacket, with the CO_2 cartridge just under the chest belt that had caused my problems. As I had a cold for the first three days, I was coughing and sneezing and compressing my chest and leaning forward each time. That had caused the CO_2 cartridge under the seat/chest belt to bruise my ribs; that's what was hurting. After releasing the seat belt and life jacket, I felt the relief of less pressure on my chest. Rest came much easier.

Carol's new Garmin 496 isn't working; our backup is out... She starts emailing friends to find a solution.

After waking to a little turbulence, I find we're just below the top of a cloud layer. I climb to 7000 then 8000 feet. Wow, amazing, we're picking up better winds. We finally see groundspeeds of 132, 137 and 146 knots. OK, that's better!

Crossing India from east to west, the winds moved to more northerly; this had been forecast on the wind charts. As we turned southwest from Nagpur to Mumbai we finally get a tailwind. Due to aggressive leaning, we used less fuel than originally planned to this point and if lower level winds are as forecast, we'll be fine. After Mumbai, we headed out over the coast and felt comfortable, only seven hours to go and plenty of fuel remaining. At 6000 feet we have crosswinds, but no headwinds and continue at 139 to 146 knots groundspeed.

Carol's friends had been at work sending recommendations for the GPS. It turned out that if the battery had been completely drained, it wouldn't always take a charge. She had to plug it in and unplug it several times. That got it set to take a charge. It started charging and working after that exercise. We were both happy to have the backup operational again, just in case.

Carol's thoughts on this leg:

Night falls once again and we are now making position reports with Mumbai Radio. The weather is great and, where there are cities, we see lots of lights and even the blinking lights of airplanes sharing the sky with us. As radio operations go, this is the most frustrating portion of the trip around the world. The HF radio is very scratchy, with lots of congestion. You can hear several layers of conversations so it is difficult to discern what voice belongs to the radio operator you wish to speak with. In addition, some aircraft operators don't pause in-between calls, so there was a constant drone of "Mumbai Radio, Mumbai Radio" on the frequency.

I was feeling pretty crabby. Being tired, listening to all of that HF-radio static, looking at a groundspeed that indicated little tailwinds, at night in the middle of an almost 20-hour flight, I felt pretty careless about radio calls, altitudes and course accuracy. I felt especially so since we weren't getting a reply light on the transponder, which meant no one saw us on their radar. In addition, I was annoyed that my brand new, expensive Garmin 496 had stopped working. I was beginning to get antsy for some real rest and less noise in my headset.

Dawn over the Indian Ocean was welcome and the coastline of the Saudi Arabian peninsula was an awesome sight, bringing relief to a bad mood. A moonscape — or the most desolate, rugged mountains of Arizona meeting the sea — is what it

looked like. Craggy brown hills with giant deltas of sand in-
between punctuated by occasional white hamlets of humanity
fringed in green under a bright sun never got boring to look at.
It was even more spectacular gazing down from the plane at
Salalah. Did someone play with white Legos? The square, light-
colored buildings surrounded by planted palm trees gave an
orderly, architectural impression from the air. The airport must
be an important place because the entrance road appeared to be
a mile long with palm trees lining the sides and the terminal
and control tower as the ending focal point. It all looked newly
constructed.

We continue the sleep shifts until dawn and we're approaching
Oman. We see brown land and hills in the distance. As we approach
the water is azure blue but all the land is brown with a few miles of
flat plain near the ocean and mountains behind. We never hear
from Sanaa Radio, Yemen airspace. But, as we get closer, we call
Salalah approach on VHF and receive a reply. He guides us in from
that point.

There is a very strong gusty crosswind and I finally land after
adding power once. The runway is long enough and a go around
isn't necessary, but wait until you see the video of that landing!!

We park as instructed, right at the back end of the ramp as far
from the terminal as possible and there isn't another plane in
sight.... The handler comes over to meet us. We're pretty tired after
another 20-hour flight.

I explain that we use avgas and that two barrels have been
ordered and are waiting for us. He explains that they come from
outside the airport and today is the first day of a four-day holiday.
It is not possible to get delivery. Another official comes with
landing and parking paperwork. We pay $16 and receive our copies.
That was quick.

Back to the main problem. Vijayan, 'Jay', is very helpful and calls
the delivery company. There is no answer. He installs us at the
terminal with instructions not to move, as he's supposed to escort us,
and then heads to his office. When he returns, he advises us that he's
reached the avgas office and they are working on our delivery. They
apparently had not received our arrival information ahead of time.

Oman arrival: Jay and other official with landing paperwork

We head to the offices below the tower to get other paperwork completed and to get our Certification of Landing signed. The hallways and offices are empty. We finally find one person, obtain the correct paperwork, fill it out and sign it. We are in another office and the tower controller walks in; there must be someone else on duty up there.... He helps us with our outbound flight plan and signs the official Certificate of Landing for us.

Then Jay leaves us with other security guards in the terminal so that he can head home, change, and get ready for an inbound flight. We sit and lie around in the boarding area, it's cold and I finally ask if I can sit outside in the sun. As I walk around to the airport gate, I notice a pickup truck outside the gate. I walk further and notice a 55-gallon drum in the back; YEAH. That's for us. I knew it was... who else would it be for?

I run back inside to inform Carol and talk with the security guard. He says yes, it's for us, but there's another problem. The driver doesn't have the permit to drive the truck on airport property. Someone else needs to be found. I knew it would all be worked out. The coffee shop opened and Carol and I had some coffee and cookies. It only takes a little coffee in these countries to wake you up; they like it strong. Me too.

Carol's Salalah observations:

Another long leg finished, and we would be done with flying over water for a while. Stepping out of the plane it was warm but the breeze that created the challenging landing was cool. Neat! This is quite a contrast from tropical Chiang Mai. We were escorted to the terminal, and my education about culturally different restroom facilities would begin. CarolAnn and I entered the ladies restroom facility together, and we each chose a door. I opened mine and found no china stool, but instead a hole in the ground and two stainless steel foot markings. How do I do this? Fortunately for me, CarolAnn had opened her door which revealed the more typical appliance, including toilet paper, and offered to switch.

As I observed from the air, the airport terminal looked new and was interesting architecturally, especially the control tower. I was looking forward to going up into the control tower to file our flight plan, get our landing paperwork signed and chat with the tower manager. It was the beginning of a holiday, so the offices were quiet as we traveled through the hall to the radar room. Jay escorted us and introduced us to the tower manager. He was wearing the traditional dress of a simple cream-colored robe with a tassel at the neck placed off to one side. I couldn't determine if the tassel was attached to a zipper or was a decoration and therefore wondered what its purpose or significance was. He was also wearing a simple pillbox style cap on his head that matched his robe and was embellished with elaborate brown embroidery. He was a man of respect and carried himself so. We reviewed a few details of the flight plan using the airway chart on the wall, got our papers signed, gave our thanks and described a little of what we were doing.

When we had the chance to talk a little about what we were doing and why, it always made an impact, people understood and became excited. Here, the tower manager was impressed and Jay, after returning from home to get ready for

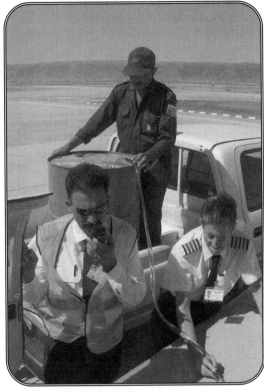

Gassing up, finally, in Salalah, Oman

his next inbound flight, reported that his two daughters wanted to know more and would be following along via the website. Even in the terminal café where we bought coffee and cookies, the shopkeeper, using broken English, communicated an admiration for our purpose and adventure. We were truly becoming a global effort.

So we waited a while longer, then signed for the fuel delivery and headed to the plane. They started making a big deal about not having the equipment to offload the avgas, but I assured them that I was equipped to do that. I had the tool to open the drum and a hose to siphon the avgas out.

It didn't take long at all. I'd already practiced in my hangar and knew the hose would siphon two gallons per minute or about half an hour for the barrel. We found out later, but didn't know at the time, that our ground crews, Norm and Flemming, had been calling and working on the gas situation as well. They were really taking care of us behind the scenes.

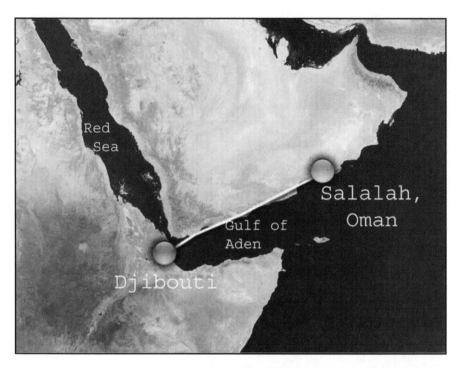

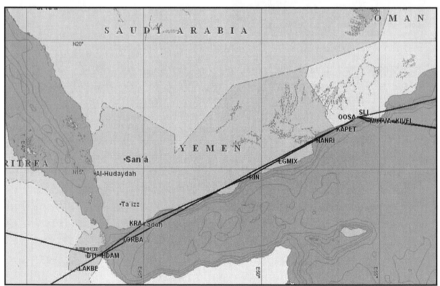

Top: Actual flight path by TracPlus Global Ltd.
Actual flight time, 5 hours 24 minutes
Bottom: Planned route across Yemen

—Leg Six—

Oman to Djibouti (080916z[7], 1:16pm local time)

Jay was off handling other arriving planes and had signed all paper-work for us to depart. As soon as re-fueling was complete, we were ready to go. Unfortunately, ATC wasn't ready. It took another 15 minutes for the tower, communicating by phone with Muscat who was working with Sanaa control (Yemen airspace), to issue our clearance to depart. Then we had to do a full departure procedure. Finally we were cruising in cool air and slowly climbing to 16,000 feet.

The airway MEA, minimum enroute altitude, is 11,000 feet. Going west, that would put our altitude at 12,000 feet.[8] However, in issuing the Yemen over flight permit, the controlling agency has required that we fly at 16,000 feet. When Bo was obtaining this permit, two days before our departure, and called me with this limi-tation, I said, "yes, we will fly at 16,000 feet." At that time, I'd say almost anything to get the permit.

Now, it was less comfortable. We were on oxygen, which was in limited supply as I didn't have an adapter to get it refilled in Thailand. The winds are worse at 16,000 than lower, so our ground-speed is 125 knots. And, it's chilly up here. After we change controllers, I ask for lower and he allows us to descend to 12,000 feet. Our groundspeed picks up to 142 knots, it's warmer, and we're happier.

We hear two "English" voices on frequency and they hear us. They ask us to switch over to frequency 123.45 to chat. It turns out that they are ferrying two Chinese planes to Uganda. They landed for fuel at Salalah just as we were departing. Now they are headed to Djibouti for the night. We talk about airspeeds, fuel capacity, and leg lengths, and then plan to meet on the ground in Djibouti.

---

7   080916z Zulu time, December 8th, 9:16am, 4 hours behind Oman time, December 8th, 1:16pm
8   Westward headings fly even altitudes while eastward headings fly odd altitudes.

Carol's thoughts:

> We are getting close to Africa, Somalia and the Gulf of Aden
> where there has been so much pirate activity. Maybe we would
> see the captured tankers and ships tied up in the distance. We
> didn't. Later, safely at home with my family over Christmas, I
> found out that this was the flight leg my mother was most
> worried about. She was afraid we would be shot down. I was
> hoping the engine wouldn't quit here as well. I really didn't
> want to be a blond pirate plaything.

We take turns resting, and then get ready for the approach.
Although these usually aren't busy airports, there are about five
airplanes all landing at Djibouti prior to sunset, i.e. within the next
hour. Each one has to do the complete arrival procedure and
approach, which means hitting the initial approach fix, turning
outbound, doing a full approach and landing. Our approach
controller keeps us up at 12,000 for what we consider too long. We
have to descend faster than normal, continue with the approach,
and slow enough to put the plane in the landing configuration.
Everything turns out well and Carol lands and turns off at the first
taxiway.

Carol's thoughts:

> It's been only us most of the way around the world and now we
> were in a group of five aircraft to do the approach into Djibouti.
> Slow down, and then speed up. It's an interesting "daisy"-
> looking arrival-and-approach procedure with long looping legs.
> Djibouti Approach keeps us really high and so it will be a slam
> dunk arrival. My friend, Paul, a previous Mooney test pilot and
> exacting instructor would be proud of my arrival, approach and
> landing.

We are signaled to parking and shutdown. Before we are out of
the cabin, the re-fueler drives up with four barrels of avgas. Now
that is service. Normally you have to go into the office and haggle
for hours to get the fuelers out. Flemming and Bo have been calling

ahead to get everything prepared. We put one 55-gallon drum into each of the rear tanks. I realize that the full amount won't be transferred, but expect to lose only a few gallons. When the operator tips the drum, I'm happy to see that he's trying to get all the avgas out.

The third drum fills the right-wing tanks and the left main; but I'm 17 gallons short on the outer tank of the left wing. I talk with Carol explaining the situation. With about 50 gallons in each ferry tank and only 17 gallons short in the wing tank, and with the normal winds over the Sahara, I'm sure we'll make it. Otherwise, we'd have to pay $710 for the last barrel and only use 17 gallons. Once it's open, you pay for it, no matter how much or little you use. She agrees that we should be OK.

Peter, one of the ferry pilots comes over and introduces himself. He wishes us well on our record attempt, and we wish him a continued good journey to Uganda. It must be a fascinating life being an international ferry pilot.

Tower at Djibouti

The handler brings the Certificate of Landing back, duly stamped and signed. These are very valuable, because without them our flight and record won't be recognized. I file it in our pouch of important and valuable documents right away. Then our handler walks us through the empty immigration and customs offices and out to the waiting bus. He explains that the bus will pick us up at 6am tomorrow morning, deliver us back here, and his helper will meet us and bring us through to the flight line. We're off.

I haven't explained that Carol's mother had made little bags for storing our various items on top of the tanks and behind the seats. We each had one for personal items, one for the electronic and battery driven equipment, one for food, one for charts and information needed for the second half of the flight, etc. At stops, we each carried one very small orange bag to our hotel. The largest item in the bag was the Freshette (female urinary relief device) that had to be cleaned after use in the plane. Besides that there was room for a toothbrush and pair of sunglasses.

Arriving at the hotel, we were too exhausted to talk with the other pilots there. I headed for my room, ordered a club sandwich, ate the French fries (as the sandwich wasn't very good) and collapsed on the bed by 7:30pm.

After our first full night's sleep in a horizontal position, I felt GREAT in the morning. Ready to GO. I showered, stretched and filled the water bottles (thinking twice that this might not be the best water to drink in the plane). I found Carol checking weather in the Internet room; she had coffee, which I promptly finished. Ahhh. The bus was there, so off we went. On the return trip, there were camels by the side of the road, so the driver stopped and Carol took some pictures.

There were tons of people at the airport; I guess the airliners must have morning departures. But, our helper got us though the lines, got our passports stamped, and out we were on the flight line. Carol headed to the flight planning office while I cleaned up the cockpit.

Within 45 minutes we were loading and firing up. I asked for taxi clearance, explaining to Carol that there would be plenty of delays and she'd have lots of time to enter the flight plan into the GPS. Of course, there were no delays and we were cleared for immediate takeoff. So it goes when you aren't in a hurry.

Carol's thoughts on Djibouti:

Good to be on the ground again and I am really looking forward to being land bound for a full twelve hours! On the bus ride to the Sheraton, I'm thinking about what I want to do. I'm tired, but not terribly so and really have the urge to see something.

The landscape is interesting. Once again the primary building materials are rock and concrete. Most of the residences and businesses are surrounded by 10'-high walls constructed of colorful rock or block with an occasional open gate to peer into. The roadway sides are mostly dirt and there is curbing bordering the asphalt. The private bus we are riding in approaches a T intersection and stops. Anyone looking in would see me with my mouth hanging open because there on the corner munching away on a lone tree is a herd of camels! Oh, I hope they will be there again in the morning so I can get a picture!

It's dark once we are at the hotel, eliminating any option of wandering about. But, in the lobby are the ferry pilots we spoke with on the radio and most of the chairs are taken up by members of the German Army. Speaking with one of the ferry pilots, I got a good review of the hotel restaurant and walked to my room trying to decide whether to be social in this faraway place or to just crater.

With a potential party in the lobby, the decision wasn't easy. I added up the negatives. I was tired and we had long legs to come. I really needed a shower. I didn't have any small, local money with which to buy beer, but, maybe I could get beer bought for me. I didn't have anything to wear, except my pilot shirt without tie and epaulets and these baggy black pants that I'd been sitting in for a long time. Yuck. And, finally, this wasn't that kind of trip. Too many negatives. So, I ordered room service, took a Tylenol PM to make sure I would sleep, cleaned out my personal bag, organized a few items for the morning and decided to set the alarm at 4:30am. Maybe I could spend an hour looking around before we headed to the airport. Room service came. I had ordered an omelet which came with French fries, a baguette and butter and some tomato soup. The food looked pretty placed on white dishes with orange linens presented on a heavy metal tray.

The alarm went off as planned and I was determined to see something of the hotel, so I got up. Padding to the bathroom I glanced at the tray which was placed next to the TV and stopped short. Fear shot up my spine as I looked at the disarray of food and thought that an animal was in my room! The remaining French fries were scattered about the tray, the salt and pepper shakers were toppled over, the dishes in a jumbled mess and the remaining baguettes strewn over the countertop. Gingerly, I walked over to the windows and moved the curtain aside. How did it get in here? Well, wait, if it was an animal everything would have been eaten and there would undoubtedly be "presents" around. I didn't see or smell any of those. Maybe a stranger came in. No, that's silly. It took splashing some cold water on my face and walking back and forth a few times to really wake up and realize what happened. I guess my real exhaustion, the timing of the Tylenol PM and the weight of the food tray caused me to plop the tray down so hard as to make everything on it fly around. Thereafter, I found my glasses, the TV changer and a book in the bed.

I'm in Africa and I want to see a little of it! Finding a lobby door to the outside, I was greeted by the sound of water lapping the shore and soft, moist air enveloped me. I was on the Red Sea! I could see the faint outline of the shore and boats bobbing in the water. Walking around the pool garden area I took in the smells, sights and sounds. I was also quiet because I didn't want to wake whomever was there sleeping in one of the lounge chairs. Walking into the lobby I tiptoed past the snoozing security guards fast asleep in opposing wing chairs. Thankfully the desk clerk was awake and I was able to buy a half hour of internet time to check the winds and weather for our next leg over Africa and to send an email out. He also brought strong dark coffee which was a treat with which to start the day. It felt really good to send a note to everyone that we were safe, doing well, and more than halfway home!

CarolAnn came in with just a few minutes left on the internet and I disappeared to gather my things to depart.

Camels in Djibouti

Scratching my ankle from the mosquito bite I got in the garden, I remembered I had better start taking those malaria pills. Driving in the bus, I was able to see the Red Sea again and wonder about the construction of the buildings and what we would see over the remainder of Africa. There they were! The camels! The driver observed my camera and stopped to escort me across the road to take a picture. The herd had wandered down the road to find another tree to munch on during the night. I wonder if their owners know where they are.

What a delight to observe others and be so privileged to be amongst a different culture. No matter where we traveled, we were treated with smiles, openness and respect. Even the burly security guards couldn't help smile and talk with CarolAnn as she practiced her French with them. At the airport we were whisked through security lines, but not before I got to see some people in their native dress. One woman wore a traditional burkha of beautiful black silk that had rhinestones lining the opening around her eyes and the bottom ends of her sleeves and hem. In contrast, another woman wore a colorful pink and yellow fabric burkha with flowers and yet another wore one with exquisite embroidery. Some of the men wore traditional robes, most being plain and light in color. On their heads they wore a simple high cap with embroidery as the tower controller in Salalah had.

I was beginning to take on a few more responsibilities and got the flight plan filled out and filed with the Djibouti official. Across Africa! Across land, we wouldn't need to wear our life vests! After a visit to a restroom I wouldn't want to visit again, we were off.

Carol in flight planning office in Djibouti

— LEG SEVEN —

Djibouti to Bamako, Mali
(090452z[9], 7:52am local time)

We took off over the water and did a slow 180-degree turn to start climbing over land; it sure was barren. We had to climb to 12,500 feet within the first hour and a half to get over the mountains. This was another combined VFR/IFR flight plan; we couldn't make the 16,000 foot altitude needed for IFR clearance. So, we departed and would climb VFR and pick up our clearance on the other side of the mountains. The weather looked good, but unfortunately, the Universal Weather flight briefing and weather package had not arrived at the handler's office. So, we didn't have wind information.

I did step climbs to conserve fuel and reduce CO emissions which had given us problems during earlier climbs. After 9500 feet, I could see the escarpment ahead and had to power climb the last 3000 feet. As we got closer, I thought we weren't going to make it, so decided to do a 360-degree turn and keep climbing. Well... we turned, but couldn't climb and turn at the same time. Aerodynamically, a little bit of lift is lost in the turn and that was enough to make the difference. Our little Lycoming engine just couldn't breathe enough of the thin air at this altitude to develop any more power, nor could our wings find enough air molecules for lift. So, we climbed straight and FINALLY made 12,500 feet, flew over the edge of the mountain, and over the plateau on top. Actually after the ridge, the land dipped down and the plateau is between 11,000 and 9000 feet. Addis Ababa, Bole International airport, is at 7,656 feet.

We flew over the VOR, just north of Addis, and outbound on the other side. It was getting cloudy and rainy and we kept maneuvering around the clouds and rain showers. From looking at a VFR chart during planning in the US, I knew there was one peak directly on our path from Addis. We kept a lookout. Finally we saw shoulders going up on both sides. The peak was under a rain shower and we

---

9   090452z Zulu time, December 9th, 4:52am, 3 hours behind Djibouti time, Dec. 9th, 7:52am

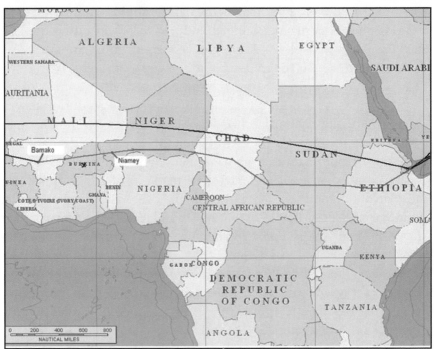

Top: Actual flight path by TracPlus Global Ltd. showing landing at
Ouagadougou. Actual flight time, 20 hours 8 minutes
Bottom: Planned route with destination, Bamako, Mali and
alternate Niamey, Niger

couldn't really see it. So, we flew around one side of it. The land sloped down after that and the weather cleared.

The winds hadn't been much help over the plateau, but I'd expected them to pick up on the other side. We descended to 8000 feet and tried to settle into our routine of emails and satellite phone messages. I'd prepared an ALS update and tried every HF mailbox on Wes' chart....no connections. I was frustrated and kept trying, but finally gave up. If the propagation wasn't with us today, there was nothing I could do about it. As both of us had slept well and felt good, we decided to do the video interview that had been pre-planned.

Phillip Hurst, founder of Air & Space Television, had done some air to air video shoots and two interviews prior to our departure. He'd given us a sealed envelope with questions. As we had Kabir's Panasonic video recorder for takeoffs and landings, we would turn that around and do a video interview using Phil's questions.

I set up the video and we did a test run to make sure we both fit in the screen, then opened the envelope and we were ON... it was FUN. We both laughed and answered the questions. Hope it's useful Phil, thanks for preparing the questions. I wish we could reproduce the CD here in this book, but the entire interview is on the CD of the flight. It was a nice "break in the action" for both of us.

I thought it was just me, the plane felt like it was surging... Then Carol said, "Do you feel that?" I did. There were very slight surges, less than 50 rpm, but noticeable and slow. After about ten or so, the engine continued as normal. Nothing more. Carol explained about a propeller governor problem she'd had one time, but the symptoms were a little different. I'd never seen or heard of anything like that. Everything was smooth now, so we just stayed vigilant and a little more on edge.

Carol's thoughts:

Flying over Africa proves to be beautiful and difficult. We get to fly a leg mostly during the day for a change and initially, we get to see the scenery up close and personal as we travel over the Ethiopian mountains. At home I love to prepare French press coffee using Ethiopian beans. They are strong and dark, brewing an excellent cup with which to wake up. As we travel over the terraced mountains, I wonder if this is where my coffee comes from. Looking for the lower mountain saddles and the ridges hiding in the rain, it's a nervous first four hours.

Once we are over the highest terrain, I think of the fun times I've had traveling the mountain west in my Mooney. It looks like the Cortez, Colorado area down there, where the rolling hills are punctuated by boulders and are intensely farmed. Beyond this terrain, it's beginning to look like Central Texas! Thoughts of home and the end of this flight begin to enter my head and I day dream of what my arrival will be like at Spicewood. I also wonder if there will be anyone to meet me in Florida. Maybe my brother will make it down from New York, or someone who has airline privileges will be able to come. I imagined searching the sea of faces for one or two that might belong to me. I've always thought it so sad to arrive at an airport and there is no one there to meet you. Unfortunately, I suspect this will be the case for me, somewhat taking the edge off of the delight of finishing and accomplishing this goal. The real end of this trip won't be until I get back to my home and see my familiar, smiling faces.

Beige, the landscape is really beige. Thinking about my question to CarolAnn over New Mexico whether or not it looked like Africa, the answer is it sort of does. A big difference is the treatment of the land. In New Mexico, there are desolate places, but the land is being ranched and people are around. Over the sub-Sahara it is desolate. The air we are flying in is dusty and smoky and you can smell it. We climb slightly to be in cleaner air not only for us, but for our engine and leading edges. What is the source of all this smoke? Looking down, I see square mile patches of black and at one point see a ten-mile long strip of fire. Wildfires are burning and there is no one to put them out. CarolAnn and I discuss this continent and all of its potentials. I hope one day all of the people here can realize their resources leading them to better lives.

It was really nice to lighten up a bit on this leg over Africa. I really enjoyed interviewing each other with the thoughtful questions given to us by folks from Air & Space Television. The trouble with the questions, however, was that now I was thinking about what food did I miss (steak and asparagus) and would I be flying anywhere again soon (yes, home). Well, it is *my philosophy that time marches on. Eventually, this leg across Africa, and this adventure would come to an end, not that it was to be endured, but instead to be savored. Every minute of it is to be savored, because upon future reflection it will have gone by so fast.*

Every time we checked, the winds were anemic, nothing, insignificant. I'd been watching them for a year and they were always howling across the Sahara at 15 to 30 knots. Today...nothing. Our ground crew emailed by Iridium satellite phone, that it didn't matter where we went, north or south, no improvement. Winds are just not there today. Oh well.

We always wrote down on the data log an estimate of when the ferry tanks would go dry so that we'd be watching the fuel pressure gauge and be ready to switch tanks right away. It's no fun when the engine coughs before you are ready. So, we'd written 2025z on our sheet using our normal eight gallons per hour estimate and planned on watching the gauge a little before.

Needless to say, we both jumped when the engine started coughing at 1648z after only ten hours and eight minutes on the rear tanks. Carol started doing calculations....that would mean we burned 10.9 gallons per hour when our previous fuel burn had always been 7.9 gallons per hours. Impossible. We didn't receive all our 55 gallons. IF our fuel burn was 8 gph, how much gas did we receive? Eighty gallons, 15 gallons short in each tank. Wow, are we going to make our destination?

We start doing calculations, looks like we're going to be 1 hour short. Bummer. No winds and not enough gas. Oh well, that's why we have alternates. We'd listed Niamey, Niger as our alternate and advise our ground crew of the situation. Since Niamey is 700 miles closer than Bamako, Mali, we had plenty of gas to make it, so we enrichen the mixture and increase our airspeed. No sense going slowly when we have our destination made and plenty of fuel.

After that, we settle down and Carol took a rest shift. I was doing satellite phone emails when one came in from Flemming:

No avgas available at Niamey Niger. We're looking at alternatives.

Flemming

I woke Carol up since she needed to be involved in this decision. I read the message we had just received. The safest thing we could do is to continue to Niamey and land. We'll figure something out from there. We backed off the power settings to conserve fuel, continued reporting to ATC, and monitored our settings and airspeeds.

We alternated flying and resting and continued through the evening into the night. It was good that we were so well rested the night before. We both felt great.

All the ground crews were working on our problem. Flemming found avgas in Burkina Faso; Bo started working on a landing permit. We had an over flight permit, but not a landing permit for that country. We did our calculations and it showed that we would only have half an hour of gas to DFFD,[10] Ouagadougou, the capital of Burkina Faso, previously Upper Volta.[11]

Our decision was to land at Niamey. We asked if car gas, high octane, was available. Universal Weather contacted their two handling agents and neither would provide car gas. I asked if they would, not as handling agents, but just a cash payment, provide several cans of car gas. The answer came back no. I knew that if we landed we could get them to help us out.

Later Bo sent an email; he had located 20 gallons of car gas at Niamey. OK, with that gas we'd make it to Bamako, Mali.

He and Flemming were still pushing DFFD, Ouagadougou, Burkina Faso. They wanted to know our decision. We restated it: plan on landing in Niamey. But, if our fuel looks good, with more than one hour remaining after calculating the flight time to DFFD, we'd continue to DFFD, otherwise we'd land at Niamey. We didn't want an instrument approach into an unknown airport, at night, with only 30 minutes of fuel remaining.

Flemming sent us the altitude descent points for the DFFD approach. Using the GPS, I zoomed in on the approach so we knew what it looked like. I drew a plan view on my knee board.

We'd backed off on power as we dropped weight from used fuel.

---

10 DFFD is the airport identifier for Ouagadougou, Burkina Faso.
11 Upper Volta. The colony of Upper Volta was established in 1919, but it was dismembered and reconstituted several times until the present borders of Burkina Faso were recognized in 1947.

We were running lean of peak. After a while, we knew we could make DFFD. We announced the decision to our ground crew and continued on. We advised ATC of our revised destination also. They had no problem.

In the middle of these diversion decisions and fuel calculations we'd also looked into N'Djamena, Chad, FTTJ, for refueling. We had both an over flight and landing a permit for Chad. But, neither Universal Weather nor Bo could get avgas confirmed, so we continued on.

We were relatively calm in the cockpit; there was not much we could do but monitor our fuel and make a decision where we would land. That wasn't the case on the ground. The ground crews made over 200 emails in several hours to get everything coordinated. It's absolutely amazing. Without the ground crew, we would not have completed the flight that evening. We'd have made it eventually, but certainly not with the ease with which everything happened that night.

Carol's thoughts:

With all of the fuel calculations and decisions of where to go and if we would we make it there, I never felt nervous. I was pleased that CarolAnn and I were pretty much always on the same page regarding safety. We could land in Niamey and just figure it out on the ground. Forget the record attempt, just as long as the result was to be able to fly again another day.

As a crew, I think we did well discussing items that came up. When I felt the surging of the engine at one point, I was waiting for CarolAnn to say something about it. When she didn't, and I was thinking along the lines of a propeller governor malfunction, a serious problem, I wanted to bring it up without creating too much of a stir. She cracked me up when she said that she thought maybe it was just her; except that now I had noticed it too, it must be there. We discussed possible causes, what to do, and we monitored it.

Probably the item that shook me up the most was each time the ferry tank ran dry causing the engine to cough and sputter. I was on high alert until the engine ran smoothly again and all of the tank valves had been put into their proper position. It wasn't until the very last leg across the Atlantic that I caught the movement of the fuel pressure gauge and we didn't have to listen to all of that sputtering. So, even though there were a few nervous moments, we would be fine.

GROUND CREW emails

CA: After our arrival in Djibouti, while we were in bed, new information came to light:

> Sent: Monday, December 08, 2008 10:02 AM
>
> Subject: FW: NOTAM[12] A0153/08 // N220FC // 108091562
>
> Hello Dash Enthusiasts!
>
> I hope you are all well. I wanted to give you a heads up on a new kink in the plans. GVAC/Sal Island just issued a runway closure notam from 0330 UTC to 1130 UTC 07-DEC to 12-DEC. We are still waiting to see a copy of the official notam.
>
> Our intrepid adventurers are due into GVAC at 0900 UTC, so they are facing a 2.5 hour delay. I'm not sure if they want to take off later from GABS or maybe HDAM. If any of you speak to CA or CF, please pass the information along. I will send them and HF e-mail as well. I know they are sleeping right now and do not want to disturb them!
>
> ETA out of HDAM is still set for 0400 UTC on 09-DEC, just FYI.
>
> Kind Regards,
>
> ~Suzanne Goldman
>
> Foxtrot Team

CA: Apparently, that night, while we were sleeping, there was already frustration, even before we departed Djibouti. Email from Bill to ground crew:

> Flemming and I spent half the afternoon ferreting out the best winds and route. We even checked to make sure that she had overflight permits for the best route. Her planned route goes about 250 miles further north

---

12 Notam. Notice to airmen, an official FAA publication of any change at airports, navigation, or other information which is essential to flight operations

than ours.

Our route shows tailwinds all the way. On hers (in addition to being 62 miles further) she'll have headwinds on part of it. Seems like a bit of a waste.

I also spoke to Universal this evening. They say that they are NOT doing any flight plans for CA. She is doing all her own routing and filing.

bill

CA: During the flight, after the ferry tanks were dry and we notified the ground crew of our revised destination, our alternate airport, Niamey, Niger, DRRN, verification started and Universal Weather found another problem.

From Suzanne:

Hello Dash ground crew/friends,

We are experiencing an issue with DRRN. The overseeing handler, Execujet broke the bad news that they do not have AVGAS. I'm working on trying to secure either high octane car gas through Execujet, or going through a different handler, Jetex for either AVGAS or car gas. Already sent a satellite e-mail to CA and CF advising them and I will keep them advised. Hopefully they aren't having problems with the sat e-mail.

I just wanted to let you all know in case DRRN falls through and we need another plan, asap. Bo, do you have a landing permit for a different country or another airport close-by that we could use as a contingency for their contingency?

I'm REALLY SORRY about all this. We originally inquired about AVGAS at DRRN back in October.

Thanks and Kind Regards,

~Suzanne

Foxtrot Team

CA: The ground crews started working on alternatives. Suzanne, Bo, and Flemming had a number of exchanges:

Suzanne,

Please try this number, can't get through from here. 234-9-7818874,5231194, this is skyrouting, handle located in Nigeria. They might be able to get us into Kano, and confirm if avgas or car gas is there.

Bo

<><>

Bo...no luck...I can't get through on either number. Will keep trying though. The lines are not so great. Any luck on your side?

~Suz

<><>

Hello Everyone—

Tarryn at Execujet S. Africa was unable to reach anyone at FTTJ.

Landover was my contact for Nigeria, but they are not based at Kano. So, maybe they do have it at Kano? Landover is not the be all end all I'm sure.

Taryn is looking at Zinder/DRZR. Not sure if it's even an a/p of entry.

Zinder is in Niger, north of Kano, Nigeria. Do y'all have any information on this airport? Agadez/DRZA is too far.

Tks,

~Suzanne

Foxtrot Team

<><>

If they turn back they have permit for possible landing FTTJ. Kano still claims they got it, but with your info I doubt it.

Bo

<><>

Bo and all-

More bad news. Our computer system just went down. I still have e-mail, but no access to our databases and trips with all of our contacts at various countries. No car gas at DRRN per Jetex AND Execujet. AVGAS/Car gas not available at any stop in Nigeria either.

Tarryn at Execujet in S. Africa is trying to help me find other locations w/ AVGAS/car gas. She's supposed to let

me know about FTTJ. If they have it, maybe CA and CF can turn around and land there.

Tks,

~Suzanne

Foxtrot

<꼭~꼭>

Dear All,

I have called Ouagadougou (DFFD) talked to the airport +226 5030 7848 who gave me this number for fuel

+226 5030 6932 as well as the mobile number of Mr. Poda +226 7024 9031.

He confirmed that Avgas 100LL is available and that the fuel guys are there H24.

May be Bo could try to organize for a landing permit in DFFD

[Pity they did not take the southern route!]

Btw, they speak better French than English there.

Let me know if you need help with phone calls.

Cheers,

Flemming

CA: Bo was able to get the landing permit for DFFD in Burkina Faso and communicated that information to us. Now it was a fuel decision; did we have enough fuel reserve to make it past Niamey, DRRN to Ouagadougou, DFFD?

From Flemming:

Hi,

I sent these messages to CA with the last 30 mins - no reply yet

FL: If not enough for DFFD, did you ask if FTTJ had avgas?

FL: FTTJ TWR is 119.7 or 118.1

FL: DRRN no avgas or car fuel, DFFD too far, intentions?

FL: Suzanne check FTTJ for avgas, unable, I tried to call unable, call N'Djamena on HF or VHF to confirm

From Bill:

> Here's the most recent transmission from flight and my reply:
>
> 30MIN RSV TO DFFD. NOT ENUF. MUST STOP DRRN. CAR GAS
>
> undrstnd.
>
> wl kp updating ETAs
>
> plnty of time 2 go.
>
> Bak tnk dry now?
>
> If not, advse when, pls.
>
> b
>
> <E><E>
>
> Hi
>
> I just got this from CA (captains choice):
>
> LAND DRRN. TRY TO BUY 5 OR 20GALL CAR GAS. CONTINU TO AVGAS STOP.All I can do is to wish her good luck with the refueling on the ground in Niamey!
>
> I do not understand why their endurance is so much shorter today.
>
> Higher power settings?
>
> Cheers,
>
> Flemming
>
> <E><E>
>
> May have found 20 gallons of car gas DRRN. Stand by and keep fingers crossed.
>
> Bo

From Flemming:

> In case they go for DFFD I sent this to CA
>
> DFFD ILS 04L OG 110.1MHz track 037 initial 2600ft 11 DME arc OG 2600ft@5DME DH: 1264ft (260 AGL) @2DME OG but the latest METAR looks OK for visual: DFFD METAR:092000Z 05001KT 6000 NSC 25/04 Q1014 NOSIG

From Bill:

> Latest transmission to flight. I'll let you know the reply.
> b
> Abeam NY 2241z 227nm @ 140kt = 1:30
> ETA DFFD 0019
> Leg tot: 19:52
> Cnfrm U wnt to cntnu to GVAC 2nite? How U guys feel?
> b

From Bill:

> Just received this message. Looks like it's going to be a long night...again.
> b   CAN MAKE DFFD. PLS TELL OTHERS

CA: Suzanne's email to everyone after the "event" sums it up:

> Hello All—
>
> Thanks for the info re routing, Flem.
>
> Indeed guys—yesterday was insane. Apologies for the drama. Paula and I were chatting last night and I confirmed with her that we WERE told that the handler at DRRN would have AVGAS for the aircraft on the evening prior to takeoff from HDAM. But, in reality DRRN had run out of AVGAS 3 days prior. When Jerri briefed me yesterday morning, she said we were just waiting for final confirmation on fuel but that everything was set verbally. So, after the ladies departed HDAM, I was fairly taken aback when we were told there was no fuel at DRRN. I guess we know now to start calling 5 days prior and call every single day thereafter to be sure it's held and confirmed for the flight!
>
> But you were all awesome and started troubleshooting and problem solving right away! Bo, when the book is published about this flight, will you please sign my copy? Flemming is right: you saved the day with setting up the stop at Ouagadougou and fuel at Niamey!
>
> Please let me know if y'all get an off time from the aircraft from GVAC!
>
> Cheers,
> ~Suzanne

I can't say thank you enough to the ground crew,
who missed more sleep than we pilots.

Night fill-up in Ouagadougou.
Thank you Lassana, Bo, and Flemming.

Back to the flight and landing in Ouagadougou:

During the approach, with power back, we felt a little surging again. Weird. Nothing major, very slight, and only a few times. I said I'd call Art, my mechanic, on the ground.

After the approach and landing at DFFD, the tower told us to park in spot 3, right beside an airliner. We got out and stretched just as Lassana from Aviation Flight Support and a guard walked up. The re-fuelers arrived at the same time. They then headed off to get their equipment.

I started filling out the paperwork and chatting with Lassana. As Burkina Faso had been a French colony, one of the official languages is French. It gave me a chance to practice the language (I'd lived in France for eight years, but had left in 1995). He explained that Bo had contacted him earlier that evening and he was happy to say, yes, they had avgas here at Ouagadougou. He had worked out the permissions and was happy to work with Bo. At that time Bo called on Lassana's phone; we chatted and I thanked him profusely for finding avgas and getting all the permits lined up. He said it had been a long night and was going to bed soon.

Carol's experience:

> *Granted, during the later part of this leg, the fuel calculations, diversion options and engine surging were foremost on my mind, but vying for first priority was my need to go and the relief tube couldn't help. For the last hour and a half, I really had to use the bathroom. After landing in Ouagadougou I politely listened to the ground personnel, another urge came and I had to interrupt to request a restroom break. I was escorted by a security guard to a beautiful FBO building, said hello to the other security personnel and headed for the ladies room. I was anticipating relief and was delighted to sit down in a clean and modern facility. But, oh no! No toilet paper. What to do? OK, I'm indeed by myself, so I'll just waddle over to the next stall and see if there is some there. Nope. Any paper towels around? No, there was just the sink with a big block of soap. I see where the towels are supposed to be. Not even anything in the wastebasket. I wish I had brought in my bag. Well, when in a different country, do what they do. Next to the toilet was a teapot shaped container full of water. So, with one hand I washed, sort of wagged myself dry and made a beeline for the sink and the soap. Seeing CarolAnn outside I mentioned she needed to bring some wiping paper in with her. It took a while on the next leg, along with the use of more hand sanitizer, to even think about eating a Power Bar.*

The fuelers returned with a large tank. We didn't need to fill the ferry tanks for such a short, ten-hour, flight to Cape Verde. So, we concentrated on the main tanks. It was a manual pump type setup, but with a meter, in litres, and normal filter and nozzle. While chatting, Lassana informed me that Bamako, Mali had run out of avgas! That was amazing....had we made it to our planned destination, we would have been stuck without being able to refuel...sometimes things happen for a reason...

It took less than 15 minutes to complete the refueling; actually longer to do the paperwork. We paid in US dollars, shook hands and were off again. That was the quickest refueling stop of the whole trip, one hour and 15 minutes. Upon departure, I had two more emails from Bo, he wasn't in bed yet....

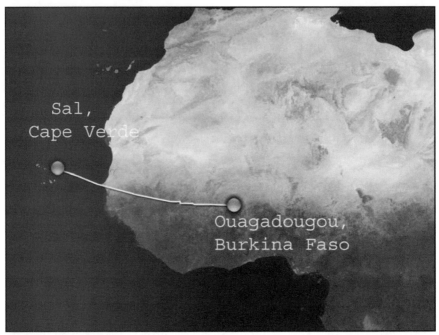

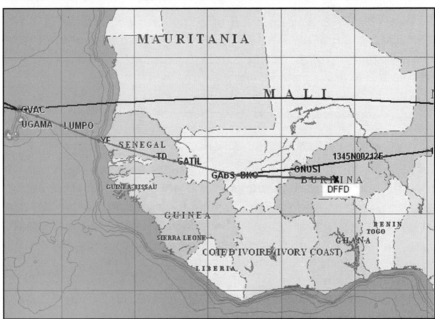

Top: Actual flight path by TracPlus Global Ltd. showing departure
from Ouagadougou. Actual flight time, 10 hours 10 minutes
Bottom: Planned route with planned departure from Bamako, Mali,
showing actual departure from Ouagadougou

—LEG EIGHT—

Ouagadougou, Burkina Faso to Cape Verde (100215z[13], 2:15am local time)

I'd tried to reach Art by satellite phone on the ground and left a message. I tried again when we were in the air and he answered. I explained the surging problem. He'd never heard of that before ....thought about it and said to call him if it happened again. He'd think about it and send an email if anything came to mind.[14] Then he asked about the runway being closed in Cape Verde. I said we hadn't heard a thing. He said it was supposed to be closed for our arrival. I said we'd check with the ground crew.

We start alternating shifts right away to stay rested. When Carol wakes up to take over, I inform her that Bamako control had given us a vector after we hit the VOR to take us around the city. We had to do a ninety degree right turn for 15 miles, then continue on course. Just after completing the detour and continuing, we received an email from ground crew, Bill, "What was THAT???" He was watching our track and thought it was some kind of avoidance maneuver. I asked about the runway closure at Cape Verde. He said is would be closed at night, but re-opened in time for our arrival.

Prior to Bamako, we'd been at 8000 feet with 23-knot headwinds. Not happy. After Bamako we descended to 6000 feet and the winds diminished; thank goodness. We didn't need to head out over the ocean to the islands of Cape Verde with headwinds and a limited fuel supply.

As the sun came up, we could see villages dotted over the brown landscape. I decided to try an HF connection and got a fast one right away. OK time to send updates.

Website update:

> A long way over Africa: Here over the very western
> portion of Africa, it's dry and dusty. Looking out the

---

13 100215z Zulu time, December 10th, 2:15am, same as Zulu time
14 Art, mechanic, was a little more worried about the surging than he let on while talking on the phone that night over Africa. He thought it was some minor contamination in the fuel, not water, but maybe diesel, kerosene or something else combustible but not avgas. We didn't have any other occurrence of surging after that leg.

window we see beige, with an occasional town, sprin-
kling of trees and dusty roads. Stops in Africa have been
interesting, especially the refueling process. Fuel has
come in 55 gallon drums on the back of a truck and
must be hand cranked to get it into the airplane. Each
fill up, at Salalah, Djibouti, and in Ouagadougou was
accomplished by airport staff, even at 2am. We have
had some drama! Headwinds over Africa had us continu-
ously calculating our fuel endurance and because of lack
of HF radio reception over most of this continent we
weren't able to get any messages out. But, we can now,
and we want to thank you for your good thoughts,
wishes and donations as we wing our way home.

Carol

We fly over hazy Dakar, the city on the western edge of Senegal.
I'd visited with friends in the early 1990s. It is really spread out with
lots of oceanfront property. Soon we were over the ocean again.
Only two hours to go to landing.

We received word that there is a fast-moving cold front headed
across Florida.

Email from Bill:

This is a message from Universal. It's a day old now so I
wouldn't act on it without an update.

Bill

A strong cold front will be approaching Florida from the
west on Thursday morning. Current models show the
strong possibility of scattered showers and thunderstorms across as early as 1000 EST over the Orlando
area and much of west central Florida. The front will
move by the area later in the afternoon which will bring
a hazard of low level turbulence associated with post-
frontal flow below FL120. Surface winds and LLWS will
be of particular concern through Thursday evening. I
would recommend an earlier arrival on Thursday
morning or a delay until Friday during the day.

Regards,

Randall Garlington

Lead Meteorologist

Meteorology and Flight Planning

Universal Weather and Aviation

Carol's thoughts:

How tired am I? This is the question to ponder as we travel to the Cape Verde Islands. I saw the line of weather heading for Florida while on the computer in Djibouti. Man, I hate it when it's been a long trip and the last part of it is the most challenging. We have had no weather at all around the entire world and now we have to deal with thunderstorms for the last landing! In the end, with the thought of how long we could get stuck if we don't beat the weather, it's time to pull out some of that pilot stuff and head home. I'm sorry because I was looking forward to staying at a nice bed and breakfast in the Cape Verde Islands, undoubtedly with a European feather bed and tasty baguettes and butter. Oh, well.

CarolAnn and I discuss our decision to continue on in regard to dealing with the weather and rest. With the Caribbean so close, I feel there are a number of options for landing if the weather causes us to turn back from Orlando, so I'm certain we can make it there. I remember a strategy for non-revenue airline flight which often works well with the weather as well. The idea is to fly as close as you can to the destination instead of making the decision not to go at all while so far away. We could at least get across the Atlantic and hopefully there would be great tailwinds to help us beat the weather.

We see the flat, brown islands in the distance. I'd read Anne Morrow Lindbergh's book, *Listen! The Wind*, about the islands and finding an air route across the Atlantic in the 1930s. I immediately knew these were the islands and remembered how harsh the conditions were when she was there.

We had a relatively strong crosswind, but Carol landed well and we parked in front of Air Luxor/Safeport. They made us welcome with coffee which tasted GREAT. The customs paperwork was quick and we were dividing duties and trying for a quick turnaround.

While Carol was working on the flight plan, I was working outside in the sun with the fuelers. Unfortunately, the fuel nozzle was larger than our hose diameter. We couldn't refuel the ferry tanks.... We looked into options. On the truck was a large funnel with filter, but its diameter was too large also. There was a smaller funnel; we started to use that, but the transfer process took too long, the funnel kept overfilling and pouring out over the plane and window. I was a little frustrated.

I suggested narrowing the diameter of the larger funnel which the ground crew did efficiently. Then we started again. It went pretty smoothly, except the person doing the hand pumping kept stopping... we were holding the funnel and nozzle in the air to let gravity drain fuel into the tank. The guy holding the nozzle would get tired and let it rest on the funnel that I was holding. I'd feel the extra weight and ask him to support the nozzle more. Then the pumper would stop pumping. Aghrrr.

We finally finished the first tank and started on the second. There was a small leak in the funnel and it was dripping down on me. Every once in a while, we'd have to stop, wring out the rags and start again. The ferry tanks were finally completed and they started on the mains. That was a piece of cake, until the delivery tank was out of gas. I'd asked for about 700 liters, doing the quick calculation in my head as we taxied in.... they'd put 700 liters in the tank and pulled it over. We were about five gallons short. After our previous gas and wind issues, I didn't want to leave without our maximum load of gas. The refueler wasn't happy, but I explained that we were crossing the Atlantic and really needed all the fuel possible.

Carol's ground time:

> *It would be my responsibility to take care of paperwork. The official landing sheet had to get to the tower for signature, and the flight plan had to be filed. In addition, I pulled copies of Orlando approaches off of the computer in anticipation of the bad weather we would find there. Finding some food for our last leg would be good too, since we had been living on Power Crunch bars and macadamia nuts. I was a bit nervous to fill out the flight plan, since it had been changed a few times and I had to calculate estimated time en route to the various waypoints across the Atlantic. This information needs to be accurate because it's the information search and rescue would use to find us. I was thinking about a small raft floating in the*

big ocean again. In addition, we were in a hurry. I welcomed the two small cups of coffee the FBO representative gave me, but it sure made me jittery.

The FBO kindly waived fees for us in exchange for information on our flight. It was great to have the internet available to print off information from our website to save these costs. Completing my work, I went outside into the beautiful day to see CarolAnn managing the fueling process. Good grief, too many helpers to actually help! Just about the time that the extra fuel came, catering came. I wish we were the big fancy jet that would have matched the catering that was delivered! The sandwiches were laid out on beautiful blue and white china dishes, there were real silverware and glasses and the fruit salad looked delicious. But, no we were sort of camping, so was there some tin foil and a plastic bag?

The gals at the FBO were so accommodating and polite. They helped at every turn and made me feel welcomed and

SafePort staff that helped us at Cape Verde

respected. Their facility is beautiful and it's another place I would like to go back to visit. Although, as CarolAnn mentioned about the Lindbergh's staying there, the wind blowing all of the time would get to be old.

While waiting for more fuel, I checked on Carol. The flight plan was done, she'd ordered catering: sandwiches, fruit and juice were being prepared. I downed a bottle of water and one of juice on the spot. It was hot on the ramp. We changed from our white shirts (with filthy collars) back to our red flight suits for the final leg home. The staff at SafePort wanted pictures with us and the plane, which we gladly obliged.

—Leg Nine—

Sal, Cape Verde to Orlando, Florida
(101513z[15], 2:13pm local time)

The last little bit of fuel was delivered and we jumped on board. A 2-hour and 45-minute turnaround. Not all that bad. We took off at 1513z, 2:13pm local time. It was a crosswind takeoff and I felt the immediate crab into the wind as we lifted off. We climbed slowly over the north end of the island and over the ocean. We were on our way home.

We leveled off at 6000 feet and I used the same power settings as on the leg to Guam. That had given us 25-hours endurance and this leg was 100 nautical miles longer. I took the first sleep shift; I was exhausted.

Two hours later I woke up refreshed; I'd really crashed and slept well. Carol's turn.

We'd started to pick up good tailwinds. I'd actually received a phone call from Flemming while we were on the ground. He said

---

15   101513z Zulu time, December 10th, 3:13pm, 1 hour ahead of Cape Verde time, Dec 10th, 2:13 pm

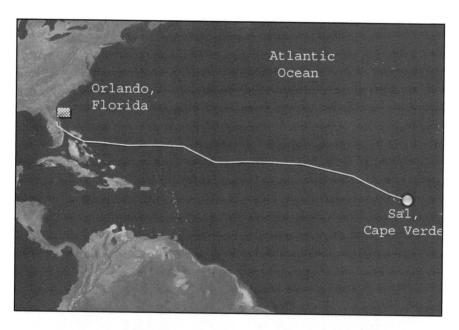

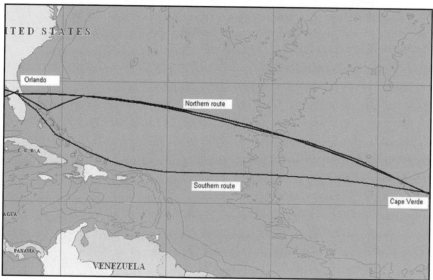

Top: Actual flight path by TracPlus Global Ltd. Actual flight time,
22 hours 39 minutes
Bottom: Optional planned routes depending on winds.

that the 25N great circle route would give us the shortest leg and best tailwinds. We'd also received another route suggestion from Bill, which tracked a little further south. We had filed an intermediate route between Bill's and Flemming's, then revised it to head further north as we progressed.

There was a little levity with the ground crew email exchanges:

From: "Bill"
To: NORMAN, Wes, Flemming
Cc: bo
Subject: exchange with crew
Date: Wednesday, December 10, 2008 12:15 PM
Exchnge with crew: (I figure that by this time, they could use a little levity)
Bill

<⅀~⅀>

TKS. LOOKING VERY GOOD. EVEN HAVE FOOD ON BOARD!

<⅀~⅀>

Food? You got food? I've been strapped to this computer for a week and Sue won't feed me.
b

<⅀~⅀>

AS WE PROGRESS & GET ETA CAN U INFORM CUSTOMS?
Yes, in the plans, will be done. Tower too. U fly - we notify.
b

<⅀~⅀>

Our ground speed increased from 141 to 146 to 153 knots. We were over 160 knots for a while. We were cheering. No stopping in the Caribbean or Bahamas for us; we were going to make it in one leg.... Fantastic.

Each of us slept well during our two hours off.

ALS update email:

> There is a terrific high pressure in the middle of the
> Atlantic giving us great tailwinds across the ocean. Right
> now we are traveling at 163 knots with a 28 knot tail-
> wind. If this continues, we'll be in Orlando at 8am, prior
> to the storm... but we'll have to see how quickly the
> storm moves through the state and how strong the tail-
> winds continue to be.
>
> We're both tired and alternating sleeping; there's no
> problem dropping off to sleep this shift. There are a few
> high clouds with bumps and rain, but with the almost
> full moon, we can maneuver around most of them.
> Mostly calm and clear.
>
> We are both feeling good and hoping to get in before
> the storm.
>
> CA & CF

Carol's thoughts:

*For me this leg is a series of sleep periods and work. The blissful
periods of sleep make the time go faster and the position reports
and hourly maintenance log keeps the mind occupied. I'm tired
and the tips of my fingers hurt from pressing all of these buttons
for the last seven days straight. When the sun rises behind us
and the clouds are illuminated with soft blue, peach and pink I
am thinking about the Caribbean, the white sands and beautiful blue waters, and how close we are to the end of our
journey. I also hear again the familiar names of US airliners on
the radio as we make our position reports as another reminder
that we are close to home.*

After 14 hours and 15 minutes the ferry tanks ran dry; great, 7.7
gallons per hour and over 11 hours remaining in the wing tanks.

The moon was smiling down on us during this leg. It had rotated
from a half moon over Guam to a full moon this night. We could
weave our way around clouds with no problem. Our communication with New York radio was simple and clear.

When I awoke, there was an unusual email from Bill:

> You are heading too far north. Are you OK? Please call.
> Bill

I thought it was a joke; Carol said that he sounded serious. So, I pulled out the intercom box, wired the headset into it, and called him on the Iridium satellite phone. He sounded tired. He had seen our deviation to the north and thought we were off course and maybe asleep. Once he saw our course head more westerly, he recognized the action we had taken; but he was still shaken.

I asked about weather in Florida. He sent us the latest forecast that showed the front would arrive slightly after our forecast arrival time. He recommended a stop in the Bahamas or Ft. Pierce. I said that we were fully rested and felt good. We'd continue on. Hopefully we'd get to Orlando before the storm, if not, we had plenty of fuel to return to Ft. Pierce. I asked him to get some sleep as there was nothing we could do for four hours and we'd need more help as we came close to Florida. We hung up with both of us feeling better.

Carol and I continued alternating flying and sleeping; we both felt good.

ALS update email:

> Hello All -
> Good crossing. Mainly clear, some puffy clouds with bumps in them. Beautiful moon guiding us home.
> GPS is showing about 5 hours to go. In 45 miles we switch from NY radio to Miami and turn a little more northeast.
> Our biggest worry is the storm headed across Florida. From ground crew reports, looks like we'll make it in before the squall line, but there will still be rain, low ceiling, and turbulence ahead of it. Our plan is to follow the route to Vero Beach; if weather is terrible, land at Ft. Pierce. If OK, continue and take a look at MCO. If good, land, if not head south and find another airport to land. We will have about 3 hours of fuel remaining at decision point.
> So, thank you all for ALL your support. The adventure is almost over; a race to the finish with a storm.
> CarolAnn

It was daylight over the Bahamas. The water color was magnificent. One controller asked what our departure point was, then what our type of plane was. He had a soft spot for Mooneys and said they are great planes. We couldn't agree more.

Carol's view:

Reaching the Bahamas, the excitement of completing this flight was tempered by the weather coming into Florida. I was quite comfortable flying up to it and hightailing away to land elsewhere if we needed to. Talking to Freeport Approach was really funny when he asked us our aircraft type, destination and departure point. I told him what we were doing and he became the first chorus of Welcome Home! that we would hear. In this area I got a few messages from home that were beginning to sound lighthearted and relieved that we almost done. I didn't relax about the weather until the Miami controller told us we would definitely beat it in.

ALS update email:

We're over the Bahamas, one and a half hours out from Orlando International. The strong cold front is moving towards Orlando from the northwest. Looks like we'll get there first, but with clouds, turbulence and rain in the area. Hopefully not thunderstorms before we arrive.

Carol is getting us on the BR65V radial to Freeport and enjoying the view of the Bahamian Islands below and through the clouds. She's feeling great about the trip but already thinking about her next one to Isle des Saints next February or March. Her butt hurts also!!

Mine hurts too, but with such a short time remaining, I'm OK with it. I'm feeling the success of the 8 day trip that gave us good weather, mostly good winds, and great supporters everywhere.

Thanks for joining along with us over the past week. The book will be out in February, so you'll be able to read ALL the details of what went on in the cockpit and on the ground. Being so busy during the flight, we gave you updates, but couldn't include all the details.

Getting the cockpit ready for landing. Thank you all again.

CarolAnn and Carol

We continued on; the east coast of Florida was clear, we could see Ft. Pierce and Vero Beach. The tailwinds, as we headed north over Florida, had us above 180 knots. The weather at Orlando International was overcast with gusty winds down the runway, but no rain and certainly no storms, yet. The Orlando forecast predicted them at 15z, in a few hours; we would arrive around 1340z. The Miami controller gave us his congratulations and told us it looked like we'd make it to Orlando with no problem. We thanked him; that was great confirmation.

We were handed over to Orlando approach who guided us up the east side of their airspace, down to 3000 feet, across the north, and on to a southwest vector to intercept the approach. We intercepted the localizer and were cleared for the approach. We were "in the soup" but focused and briefed. It was a little turbulent, but not too bad. Carol saw the ground, then, at 1200 feet, we were below the clouds with the runway two miles straight ahead. Tears came to my eyes and I fought them back. Not before landing.

The tower controller cleared us to land and congratulated us. As we landed my eyes welled with tears. Tower said we could turn off "anywhere we wanted." We headed to customs. Flight time: 22 hours, 39 minutes.

Carol's thoughts:

> Welcome Home! I wasn't ready to believe it until the wheels were on the ground in Orlando. The approach to intercept the ILS seemed to take forever. Rocking and rolling through the clouds, CarolAnn did a great job, and I felt calm on the radio accepting congratulations on the completed flight. I began to wonder if I would see anyone familiar.
>
> Oh, CarolAnn, you deserve a good cry! I am so proud of you and what you have done, at awe and feeling so privileged to have been a part of this effort! I won't be able to adequately express my gratitude for taking me on this marvelous, well executed adventure. Champagne! We deserve Champagne! I touched the Lucky Lindy coin in my pocket, made a note of our engine shut down time and smiling, got out of the plane.

A Galaxy Aviation golf cart guided us to Customs and chocked us. The customs official came out and we handed him our passports. He said we must have had some help because he had all the clearance documents ahead of time and everything was in order. He congratulated us on our record flight. I pointed to Galaxy Aviation, behind him, and said the champagne was over there.

He said, "I don't want to get between you and the champagne," he pulled our chocks and we fired up one last time and taxied 200 yards to the Galaxy ramp.

There were banners, TV cameras, reporters and tons of friends. The storm had stopped more from flying in for our arrival. We hugged and ate ice cream (thanks Debey) and hugged and took pictures and hugged some more. Tom opened a bottle of champagne and started to pour it over me. I got the bottle and took a drink; that was success. Carol took it and also poured it over me.....then took a drink. With the storm, there was no way we would fly home, so a little champagne was a great way to end the trip and start the day.

Finally we were herded inside to be interviewed by two TV stations and other reporters. More pictures, interviews. Oh yes, we'd left a bag at Galaxy, so we got to change our T-shirts, wash up a little, brush our teeth, and feel better!

Finally it was over and we were driven back home. Bill had brought his plush motor home down for our return trip. What luxury. Actually we talked the whole way home and didn't use the shower or bed. He drove through the storm; it was pelting down. We sure were glad we'd made it to Orlando before it did.

After being deposited at my house, we got four hours sleep before the welcome home party thrown by the neighborhood. There were about 100 people waiting for us. We were bleary eyed but happy. There were cookies, a cake, coffee, champagne and lots of people, waiting to hear about the trip.

After the initial hugs and congratulations, I asked for a microphone and said we'd tell a few stories. Well an hour later my neighbors were the first group to get the "info dump" and all the choice stories from the adventure. Wes was there and he was able to fill in the ground crew portion of what was going on over Africa. We wished someone had videotaped it; because we'll never be able to tell it like that again. Exhausted, euphoric, a little bit tipsy from champagne and no food, we kept going and going.

Neighbors Ellen and Peter invited us to supper.... I hadn't thought about eating; great idea. Many thanks!! That revived us enough to make it home and sleep.

Carol pouring champagne over CarolAnn.
Photo by Joe Burbank, reprinted with approval
from the Orlando Sentinel

EPILOGUE

I'd lost five pounds; Carol had lost seven pounds. Carol flew her Mooney back to Texas on Saturday, December 13, 2008, to her friends, reporters, and parties.

I didn't realize what it had taken out of me. I didn't sleep correctly for four nights. Finally the fifth night I dreamed and when I awoke, I knew I'd dreamed. Finally I'd had a good solid night's sleep. I was on the road to recovery. Tuesday, I felt better and on Wednesday, the sixth day after our return, I finally felt normal, 100% normal again.

The record is unofficial; I sent all the certificates to Art at the National Aeronautic Association on Monday, December 15th. My calculations have us at 115 mile per hour. I'll await the final calculation. Every time I think about it, I smile. It's over, I can rest now. After 18 months of preparation and eight and a half days of flying, we did it!

But, we didn't make any headlines, we didn't get national TV attention, we didn't get acknowledged by AOPA[*] on their weekly email information updates (they did write a very complete article two weeks after our flight). We didn't get any major donations for ALS. I am disappointed in the coverage and donations. Friends and pilots everywhere donated and the fund total after the flight is at $153,000. But, that's a far cry from where we expected to be.

Our objective to set a new world speed record, westbound around the world, was achieved and the old record was smashed. Our objective to raise awareness and donations for ALS research is still underway.

This book will go a long way to increasing donations. Thank you for buying a copy and donating to ALS. If you are enjoying reading a friend's copy, please order your own or donate. We'll be making hundreds of presentations over the next two years. Then it'll be time to move on.

---

[*] AOPA Aircraft Owners and Pilots Association

My third world trip is planned in my head. June 2010, fly down to Brazil for the next Earthrounders meeting. After that, cross the Atlantic and head to Norway. As the weather gets cooler, start moving south until I reach South Africa; then fly north and east again. Madagascar, Mauritius, Seychelles, India, Thailand; a LONG stop in Thailand. As it cools off again, head south to Australia and New Zealand. Then across the South Pacific. Southern Chile and Patagonia are on my list, then a leisurely trip north and back to Florida. Then I'll settle down. Promise.

Carol's final thoughts:

I was fortunate to have had several welcome homes. The initial gathering in Orlando comprised of new acquaintances, back at Spicewood, were my friends and in New York, my family. It wasn't until I got home that I realized what I did. There have been a few disappointments with the media and the economy impacting our ability to raise the funds we would have liked. But, I will keep trying. As I talk about the flight, I hope it inspires others to make a goal and strive for it, regardless of what anyone thinks and how impossible it seems.

When I got to Spicewood and was able to tell the gathered aviators and friends about the trip, my first statement was that I didn't need to tell them anything, because they were all there with CarolAnn and me, crammed into that little airplane. They really were! If they weren't in the cockpit, then they were holding up the wings. It's a positive energy thing. They laughed over some of the stories and slowly they began to tell me some of their own tales of following us around the world.

Getting to hug my family, especially my mother, was grand. She really didn't want me to go on this adventure. I thought about her worrying about me the entire time, but finally accepting my desire to go do this. I'm glad that CarolAnn made the comment that she was becoming attached to her personal orange bag that my mom sewed.

Thank you, CarolAnn for dragging and mentoring me around the world. I think we made a good crew and it will take a long time to really internalize what we did. It was a life changing adventure and I hope one day I will be able to offer an opportunity to someone as you have generously handed this one to me.

Finally, in the spirit of the family that decided that the "Dash for a Cure" should be the charity to benefit from their Christmas brunch, may we volunteer ourselves to positively make a difference. I have seen first hand that smiles and open attitudes are returned around the world.

As this book goes to press, we received word from the National Aeronautics Association that they will be certifying the record within the next two days.
The calculated speed is 115.35 miles per hour.

Chip's sister, Cheryl, welcomes
and congratulates Carol
on a successful flight.

REFERENCES

Weather web sites:
http://aviationweather.gov and go to Satellite - Intl on the left hand side
http://www.goes.noaa.gov

FAA information on countries and airports:
www.faa.gov/ats/aat/ifim/ifim2tc.htm

Web site for this flight:
www.alsworldflight.com

CarolAnn's 2003 world flight:
www.kerrlake.com/mgarratt

Other earthrounder flights:
www.earthrounders.com

ALS web site:
www.als.net

THANK YOU, DONORS AND SPONSORS

StarPort Cambata Aviation
Ken Melanson
Chip and Jan Gulden
Universal Weather
Fusion PR
Winslow LifeRafts
Aircraft Spruce
Scheyden Precision Eyewear
Care Jet
Champion AeroSpace
General Aviation Modifications, Inc.
Concorde Battery
Oregon Aero
Iridium Satellite LLC
Arctic Air
Aerial Spins
Magnum Engines
Challenger Aviation Products
Jeppesen
Mooney Aircraft Pilots Association
BNRG, Power Crunch
SPOT
Exxon Oil

The hug that went around the world

Debey gives CarolAnn a hug in Orlando. This is to be given to Gary in San Diego. Gary was Debey's mentor pilot and friend.

Upon arriving in San Diego, CarolAnn gives Debey's hug to Gary. In return, Gary gives CarolAnn a hug for Debey for her successful completion of her private pilot license. (no photo)

CarolAnn carries this hug around the world and, upon returning to Orlando, she gives Gary's hug to Debey.

GLOSSARY

ADF: Automatic Direction Finder. A piece of radio navigation equipment in the airplane that senses and indicates the direction to the non-directional beacon (NDB) ground-based transmitter.

Angel Flight: Not-for-profit organizations throughout the US that offer free transportation to those with medical needs that cannot be met in their local area.

ATIS: Automatic Terminal Information Service. The continuous broadcast of recorded non-control information in selected terminal areas. This usually gives weather, airport conditions, and expected approaches in use, and it is updated hourly.

Camelbak: Brand of hydration system. A backpack with water bladder and hose, usually used by hikers and bikers for quick and easy hydration.

DAR: Designated Airworthiness Representative. FAA-appointed specialist who, under the guidance of an FAA advisor, can make certain approvals.

DME: Distance Measuring Equipment. A piece of equipment in the airplane used to measure the nautical-mile distance from the plane to the emitter on the ground, based on the frequency dialed in.

EAA: Experimental Aircraft Association. A group dedicated to homebuilt aircraft, restoring aircraft, and helping members to build their own planes.

FBO: Fixed Base Operator. A business based at an airport that provides services, fuel, etc. for local and transient aircraft.

FIR: Flight Information Region. An airspace of defined dimensions within which Flight Information Service and Alerting Service are provided. For instance, Oakland Radio FIR covers from the coast of California to 05S latitude. Auckland Radio covers most of the South Pacific.

Flight Aware: Internet site that tracks and gives ETA for flights in the US under instrument flight rules.

GA: General Aviation. That portion of civil aviation which encompasses all facets of aviation except air carriers holding a certificate of public convenience and large aircraft commercial operators. GA covers most small, private planes and company jets.

GAMI: General Aviation Modifications, Inc. is an aftermarket manufacturer of fuel injector nozzles, GAMI injectors, that modify the fuel injected into each cylinder to improve the fuel/air ratio for smoother and more consistent operation with less fuel consumed.

HSI: Horizontal Situation Indicator. Navigation avionics that have a remote compass and can be connected to a GPS.

IFR: Instrument Flight Rules. Rules governing the procedures for conducting instrument flight; this covers altitudes, airways, communication, etc.

ILS: Instrument Landing System. Precision equipment permitting a pilot to descend through clouds down to 200 feet over the runway to make an approach. This is the most precise approach for general aviation pilots.

IMC: Instrument Meteorological Conditions. Meteorological conditions expressed in terms of visibility, distance from cloud, and ceiling less than the minima specified for visual meteorological conditions.

LLWS: Low level wind shear.

LOC: Localizer. One component of an ILS, which provides course guidance to the runway.

LOP: Lean of Peak. Running the engine leaner, less fuel, than that necessary at peak exhaust gas temperatures.

METAR: Aviation Routine Weather Report. This gives the weather report for a specific airport at a specific time. It includes the wind, visibility, cloud cover, temperature, dew point, and altimeter setting.

Monroy Tanks: Extended range tanks, adding 34 gallons outboard of the standard wing tanks, in Mooney aircraft. These are named after their inventor, José Monroy.

Notam: Notice to airmen, an official FAA publication of any change at airports, navigation, or other information which is essential to flight operations

Oregon Aero: Company that re-upholsters or provides new aircraft seats that incorporate improved back support and cushioning to prevent and eliminate pain.

Over Gross: Each plane has a design maximum gross weight, over which it is illegal and irresponsible to operate the plane. With an FAA endorsement and specific requirements, it is possible to legally operate over gross weight.

SAR: Search and Rescue. If a flight plan has not been closed within a specified time, a search-and-rescue operation will be initiated to find the pilot and plane. This service seeks missing aircraft and assists those found to be in need of assistance.

Sun 'N Fun: Spring Air Show held in April each year in Lakeland, Florida.

TAF: Terminal Aerodrome Forecast. Aviation weather forecast for a given airport. For a specific airport and valid period of time, this gives the forecast conditions of wind, visibility, and cloud cover.

Transponder: Aircraft avionics receiving a signal from the ground and sending a reply signal with location and altitude.

Unicom: A non-government communication facility which may provide airport information at certain airports.

UTC: Universal Coordinated Time, also known as zulu time. The standard time in Greenwich, England. Used for all aircraft departure, en route, and arrival times, worldwide.

VFR: Visual Flight Rules. Rules that govern procedures for flight under visual conditions. Also used to indicate weather conditions greater than minimum VFR requirements.

VOR: Very-high-frequency Omni-directional Range. Radio signal output giving the pilot 360-degree indication of his position relative to the beacon.

Young Eagles: Program by EAA to give youngsters from ages 8 to 17 an introduction to aviation for free.

Zulu time: Also know as UTC, universal coordinated time, see above.

Carol and CarolAnn
telling stories of the flight

I offered the opportunity to over a dozen teachers to talk with their students, using the Iridium satellite phone, while we were flying. I requested that they explain to the students ahead of time what we were doing and follow us on the Internet. We would set up a schedule and call them from different locations around the world. We could talk about geography, history, aviation, weather, whatever they wanted, and answer questions from the students.

Only four teachers took me up on this offer. As it turned out, due to our schedule, this was all we could handle and I still had to postpone one set of phone calls for a day. But we were able to call all the schools, talk with the teachers, and answer the students' questions.

It was a highlight for both Carol and me. Each time, after we "hung up" the phone, we were all smiles. The students' questions were outstanding. They were interested in what we were doing, had tried to figure out what it felt like to be in such a small space for such a long time, and had questions on the weather, altitudes, bumps, what we could see, as well as many others that we would never have thought of.

Carol and I both wanted to be an inspiration to others through this flight. We thank the teachers and principals who allowed the time and prepared their students to participate. We hope that someday a few of these students will have an amazing adventure of their own.

How to Obtain Additional Copies of

Upon Silver Wings II: World-Record Adventure
and/or
Upon Silver Wings: Global Adventure in a Small Plane

Books may be ordered three ways:

1. Please send a minimum contribution of $25 (for each book) to cover shipping and handling ($30 for overseas donations) to ALS-TDI.

   a. Telephone: 617-441-7270, please have your credit card ready.

   b. Send check, payable to ALS-TDI to 215 First St., Cambridge, MA 02142. Please write **Silver Wings** on the envelope and memo section of your check.

2. To receive an AUTOGRAPHED copy, please send a minimum contribution of $35 ($40 for overseas donations) to ALS-TDI and receive a book signed by the author and a confirmation of your tax-deductible contribution.

   a. Telephone: 617-441-7270, please have your credit card ready.

   b. Send check, payable to ALS-TDI to 215 First St., Cambridge, MA 02142. Please write **Silver Wings** on the envelope and memo section of your check.

   Please note: Contributions made directly to the ALS Therapy Development Institute in excess of $25 will be tax deductible to the extent allowed by law. All revenue will go directly to ALS-TDI.

3. Amazon.com

   When you buy from Amazon.com, 15% of the list price goes to Amazon as commission and the remainder, minus shipping and handling, goes to ALS-TDI. These purchases are *not* tax deductible.

SHARE THIS PAGE WITH SOMEONE WHOSE LIFE HAS BEEN TOUCHED BY ALS.

ALS
Amyotrophic Lateral Sclerosis
Motor Neurone Disease (MND)
Lou Gehrig's disease

ALS is a chronic, progressive disease that is marked by gradual degeneration of the nerve cells in the central nervous system that control voluntary muscle movement. The disorder causes muscle weakness and atrophy which paralyzes the entire body, yet leaves the mind untouched. The vast majority of ALS patients die within two to five years of diagnosis. There are no effective treatments and there is no cure.

There are an estimated 30,000 ALS patients in the US today with over 5,600 new patients diagnosed each year. ALS has roughly the same incidence rate as Multiple Sclerosis. Statistically, someone you know will contract ALS in the next ten years.

Most people who develop ALS are between 40 and 70 and it is 20% more common in men than women. Lou Gehrig, with whom ALS is most commonly associated, first brought national and international attention to the disease back in 1939 when he abruptly retired from baseball after being diagnosed with ALS. However, ALS is not just Lou Gehrig's disease and it knows no boundaries. The disease has cut short the lives of such notable and courageous individuals as Hall of Fame pitcher Jim "Catfish" Hunter; creator of Sesame Street, Jon Stone; actor, David Niven; Senator Jacob Javits; and most recently Tom Watson's golf caddy, Bruce Edwards.

ALS Therapy Development Foundation is a nonprofit biotechnology company focused on finding treatments and a cure for today's ALS patients. It was founded by the brother of a patient with ALS. A number of scientists and associates who work for ALSTDF have been motivated by a loved one with the disease. Please donate today.